s u j e t s   e t   m o d è l e s
d e   c o r r i g é s

ANNALES BEP/CAP tertiaires 1994

Anglais

Avec la collaboration de
Jean-Paul Pouderon
Professeur de lycée professionnel hors classe

vuibert

ISBN : 2-7117-**9305-2**

ISBN : 2-7117-9305-2

Avertissement

Les nouvelles dispositions réglementaires prévoient qu'une même épreuve peut servir à évaluer les candidats en vue de la délivrance du BEP rénové et du CAP intégré.

C'est la raison pour laquelle les vingt épreuves que nous avons sélectionnées présentent une double grille de barème. Souvent, et ce point est important, les candidats au CAP ont un nombre moindre de tâches à réaliser, et la pondération de chaque exercice est différente. Dans des cas moins fréquents, un exercice spécifique au CAP se substitue à un exercice plus difficile réservé au BEP.

Sommaire

2e partie – Corrigés

3e partie – Glossaire

Observations et conseils

Le présent ouvrage regroupe une sélection de vingt épreuves écrites d'anglais destinées aux candidats du BEP et du CAP du secteur tertiaire et hôtelier. Pour quinze d'entre elles, nous proposons des corrigés complets agrémentés d'indications précises de nature à guider l'élève et à modeler ses réflexes.

Mais, avant de se glisser dans l'étude détaillée de ces documents, il est utile de dégager préalablement de l'ensemble des tendances générales, dans le sens d'une étude typologique des supports utilisés et des thèmes, ou bien vers une étude typologique des exercices recensés.

Supports et thèmes

Les supports

Parler ici de « supports » plutôt que de « textes » est judicieux tant il est vrai, que des photos, des dessins, des tableaux, des plans, des graphiques, des pictogrammes complètent ou se substituent parfois aux textes traditionnels. Ces supports sont souvent une aide, car ils balisent rigoureusement le parcours du candidat que la courte durée de l'épreuve – une heure seulement – met dans l'obligation de réagir vite et dont l'imagination peut être mise en panne sèche par la situation d'examen. Mais ils peuvent ici ou là poser problème lorsque, au-delà des difficultés purement linguistiques, ces supports se prêtent eux-mêmes à des interprétations hésitantes de la part du candidat.

L'image sert souvent de point de départ à une description, ou élucide une situation qui servira de cadre à un dialogue. Les pictogrammes – signes figurés ou symboliques représentant une notion, une activité... – mettent le candidat en posture d'utiliser un certain vocabulaire spécialisé. Les graphiques l'orientent plutôt vers l'emploi des comparatifs, des dates, des quantificateurs, vers l'expression de la durée.

Quant aux textes proprement dits, qu'ils soient dialogues, textes narratifs, textes descriptifs ou textes argumentatifs, ils dépassent rarement deux cents mots. Ils fournissent aux candidats avisés un gisement précieux où puiser éléments lexicaux et tournures grammaticales en soutien de leur production personnelle.

Les thèmes

Ces supports, qu'ils soient textuels ou iconographiques, peuvent se répartir dans les épreuves d'examen qui font l'objet de ce recueil selon trois grandes orientations thématiques :

1. *Hôtellerie/Restauration :*

– accueillir, proposer, servir,
– ustensiles de cuisine, vaisselle, couverts,
– équipement hôtelier et de restauration,
– services hôteliers, personnel,
– nourriture, boissons,
– loisirs, tourisme.

2. *Secrétariat/Bureautique :*

– matériel de bureau traditionnel (machine à écrire, classeurs, bureau, etc.),
– équipement bureautique moderne (ordinateurs, imprimantes, traitement de texte...),
– activités de secrétaire (téléphone, courrier, organisation...),
– vie de l'entreprise, personnel de l'entreprise,
– argent / banque / comptabilité.

3. *Thèmes généraux*

Nous entendons par là les questions liées à la vie quotidienne et à l'actualité :

– le monde du travail,
– le monde des loisirs,
– la culture des jeunes (sports, musique, mode...),
– l'argent,
– les moyens de transport,
– vie en ville / à la campagne,
– les questions humanitaires : racisme, toxicomanie, violence, guerre...

Types d'exercices et conseils

Les exercices relevés dans les épreuves qui nous concernent obéissent tout naturellement aux trois grands objectifs fondamentaux que sont :

– la capacité à comprendre un message écrit en anglais,

– la capacité à construire correctement une phrase,

– la capacité à formuler de façon autonome un message en anglais.

Même si en aucun cas l'exercice de l'une de ces capacités n'est possible sans la mise en jeu au moins partielle des deux autres, du moins peut-on mettre à jour ces dominantes à l'écart de toutes les imbrications possibles par souci de clarté.

Compréhension

Ce type d'exercices est logiquement toujours le premier proposé. On le trouve sous les formes suivantes :

• Right or wrong ? / True or false ? / Yes or no ? Ces exercices à système binaire sont maintenant systématiquement enrichis – on comprend aisément pourquoi – de l'obligation faite au candidat de justifier sa réponse par une phrase complète ou une expression tirée du texte.

Conseil : veiller à ne pas tronquer la structure de phrase nécessaire tirée du texte pour ne pas la dénuer de sens.

• Choose the right answer / Tick the right statement. Voilà le bien connu questionnaire à choix multiple qui propose au candidat de cocher la bonne réponse dans une série. Cette tâche dans laquelle l'élève se sent souvent à l'aise présente cependant la difficulté suivante : les propositions erronées sont souvent proches par quelques mots de la tournure de référence du texte.

Conseil : faire en conséquence une lecture précise, prudente et attentive.

• Who ? What ? Why ? Where ? How ? How long... Cette gamme maintes fois utilisée se monte en allant du général au particulier, de la compréhension globale à la compréhension détaillée. À noter toutefois qu'elle a un niveau d'exigence linguistique supérieur aux formes précédentes.

Conseil : répondre par des phrases complètes (sujet + verbe + complément) ; être attentif au temps utilisé dans la question que l'on reprendra vraisemblablement dans la réponse.

• **Translate into French**. L'exercice de traduction en français, autrement dit, la version, est par excellence un exercice de compréhension, mais il ne faut jamais perdre de vue qu'il se double d'une autre exigence, à savoir la capacité à s'exprimer de façon précise et correcte... en français. Signalons que le passage à traduire n'excède jamais les trois ou quatre lignes.

Conseil : gardez-vous des non-sens au moins aussi lourdement pénalisés que les contresens.

Exercices grammaticaux

Il n'y est pas question de références grammaticales théoriques. En revanche, les compétences recherchées sont mises en œuvre dans des exercices très ciblés à travers lesquels le candidat est invité à résoudre un arcane grammatical particulier, en situation.

• **Fill in the blanks / Find the missing word**. Ces exercices lacunaires, dits « à trous » dans le jargon scolaire, conviennent particulièrement à vérifier la maîtrise de l'emploi des temps et de leur aspect.

Conseil : tenir compte des indicateurs temporels, adverbes, locutions, compléments circonstanciels de temps.

• **Choose the right word**. Voici réapparaître la formule des réponses à choix multiple au service cette fois-ci de la noble cause grammaticale.

• **Ask or answer**. Les jeux de question/réponse permettent de vérifier la maîtrise de la phrase interrogative et affirmative. L'exercice **Find the corresponding question** en est l'avatar le plus réaliste et le plus exigeant, dans lequel le candidat est poussé à se remettre dans une situation de dialogue. On attend alors de lui la connaissance des mots interrogatifs simples *(who ? what ? where ? how ? whose ?...)*, mais aussi composés *(how far ? how much ? what.. to ? where... from ?)*.

Conseil : les questions portent sur les mots soulignés.

Expression

Entendons, par là, la production d'un message plus élaboré où le fond se sert de la forme. Cette production écrite peut être soit dirigée, soit plus ou moins personnelle.

• **Le thème d'imitation** est un exercice de traduction du français à l'anglais dont la difficulté est atténuée par le fait que les tournures à utiliser ou les mots utiles se trouvent déjà disséminés dans le texte de l'épreuve.

Conseil : avant de céder au découragement, passer une nouvelle fois par une lecture sélective du document.

• **Le développement personnel/l'essai.** Il s'agit d'une formule où le candidat peut davantage exprimer son sentiment personnel, ses expériences. Il est invité à s'exprimer sur un sujet qui demeure naturellement dans la thématique du texte de l'épreuve. Le nombre de mots attendus est souvent indiqué. Il n'excède pas soixante, en général, autrement dit huit à dix lignes. Si aucune indication n'est donnée, doser le temps à consacrer en fonction du nombre de points attribués au barème.

Conseil : ne pas croire que la quantité fasse seule l'affaire ! On tiendra compte de la correction des phrases, de la richesse lexicale, de la variété des tournures, des liens logiques qui organisent l'expression.

Avant de rédiger, le candidat doit s'attacher à comprendre le type de texte que l'on attend de lui. Est-ce un texte descriptif (commentaire d'une image...) ?, un texte narratif (récit d'une expérience...) ?, un dialogue ?, un texte argumentatif (débat, opinion...) ? Dans chacun de ces cas de figure, le profil linguistique sera différent :

– dialogue →
- tournure interrogative,
- *short answers ; question tags,*
- formules de politesse, etc.

– récit →
- *simple past/past continuous,*
- indicateurs temporels,
- expression de la durée, etc.

– description →
- *there is, there are,*
- présent,
- indicateurs spatiaux, etc.

– argumentation →
- liens logiques,
- expression de la cause,
- but,
- conséquence,
- souhait, volonté.

Ces conseils généraux éclaireront peut-être un peu les pas des candidats dans leur marche vers l'examen. Les corrigés des exercices d'expression sont ponctuellement précédés de conseils sous l'appellation d'aide méthodologique, d'aide grammaticale et d'aide lexicale. Ce recueil n'étant pas destiné à se substituer à une grammaire, nous nous contentons d'indiquer les prérequis en jeu dans l'exercice proposé. De même, le lexique thématique auquel nous adressons le lecteur en fin d'ouvrage ne saurait remplir, avec moins de trois cents mots, le rôle d'un dictionnaire. Bonne route !

Index thématique

Avertissement : *de nombreux textes ou supports d'épreuves ne comportaient pas de titre. Par commodité, nous avons pris la liberté de leur en attribuer un.*

Organisation des textes par académie

Pages	Titres	Académie	Spécialités	Thèmes	Corrigés
19	Eating habits	Aix-Marseille	Hôtellerie/Restauration	Habitudes alimentaires	+
39	Sound idea	Amiens	Secteur tertiaire BEP/CAP	Bureautique, matériel	+
21	Welcome to the Patras Hotel	Amiens	Hôtellerie/Restauration BEP/CAP	Menu/Services hôteliers	
23	A guest is a guest	Bordeaux	Hôtellerie BEP/CAP	Confort hôtelier/Équipement	-
64	A French doctor	Caen	Dactylo BEP/CAP	Aide humanitaire	-
27	La Reine Mathilde Restaurant	Caen	Hôtellerie/Restauration BEP/CAP	Menu de restaurant	+
47	Dear Sir	Corse	ACC/CAS/ESAC BEP/CAP	Secrétariat (activités)	-
30	Wine district	Corse	Hôtellerie-Restauration BEP	Les vins	+
45	Talking telephones	Grenoble	Tertiaire BEP/CAP	Répondeurs téléphoniques	+
41	A byte at the restaurant	Lille	Tertiaire BEP/CAP	Bureautique, ordinateur	+
67	« Air » Jordan	Lyon	Tertiaire BEP/CAP	Vedettariat	+
32	The Hard Rock Café	Lyon	Hôtellerie/Restauration BEP/CAP	Garçon de café/Serveur(se)	+
50	Harrods account card	Nantes	Tertiaire/Alimentation/Hôtellerie CAP/BEP	Carte de client privilégié	+

Pages	Titres	Académie	Spécialités	Thèmes	Corrigés
43	Toshiba notebooks	Nice	CAS/ACC/ESAC/Hôtesse BEP/CAP	Bureautique, matériel	+
72	Danger, baby food	Montpellier	CAS/ACC/ESAC BEP/CAP	Terrorisme	-
60	Working holidays	Orléans/Tours	CAS/ACC/Distr.-Mag.	Travaux saisonniers	+
34	At the restaurant	Orléans/Tours	CAP/BEP Hôtellerie/Restauration	Serveur	+
53	British banks	Poitiers	CAS/ACC BEP/CAP	Argent de poche	+
58	Keeping the workers at work	Polynésie	BEP/CAP	Absentéisme des travailleurs	+
69	This boy is just four, but...	Rennes	Secteur tertiaire	Vedettariat précoce	-
74	British people and holidays	Rennes	Secteur tertiaire	Vacances et chiffres	-
55	There's nothing to keep youngsters here	Strasbourg	ACC/CAS/Distr.-Mag. BEP/CAP	Désertification rurale	+

SUJETS

HÔTELLERIE-RESTAURATION

Aix-Marseille

1

THÈME ABORDÉ	SPÉCIALITÉS
Eating habits	Hôtellerie-Restauration Options Cuisine-Restaurant

EATING HABITS HAVE CHANGED IN BRITAIN

Thirty years ago, the British consumed more sugar and butter than they are consuming now. Hamburgers and chips or sausages and chips are children's favourite dishes of course, but older teenagers and families are eating more dietetic food : less butter, less fat, less sugar, less meat, more fruit and vegetables and more fish.

People are drinking much more fruit juice than they did ten years ago, and the consumptions[1] of milk, tea, coffee and... beer are less important.

The British also eat differently : meals are smaller. Half of the adults have one real meal a day, eating snacks the rest of the time. Snacks (sandwiches – cake – chocolate bars...) aren't good for your health, because they contain too much fat, sugar and salt, and they are poor in vitamins and fibre. What we need, on the opposite, is a healthy diet with varied and proper meals.

As for[2] the big traditional English breakfast, with eggs and bacon, it is almost[3] a thing of the past.

1. *consumption :* consommation. 2. *as for :* en ce qui concerne 3. *almost :* presque.

QUESTIONS

I. Choisissez la bonne réponse, puis justifiez-la (BEP 4 pts, CAP 8 pts). Attention : Une réponse non justifiée (même s'il s'ajit d'un *right*) ne sera pas prise en compte :

1. British children don't like hamburgers and chips.

Right. ....

Wrong. ....

2. British people drink more beer, milk, tea and coffee than before.

Right. ....

Wrong. ....

3. 50 % of the adults have a real meal.

Once a day.
Twice a day.
Three times a day.

....

4. Snacks are not healthy food.

Right. ....

Wrong. ....

II. Répondez aux questions suivantes (BEP 6 pts, CAP 2 pts) :

1. Why were family meals in Britain less dietetic thirty years ago ?

2. Do a lot of people in Britain eat bacon and eggs for breakfast today ? Justify your answer.

3. Do you think your food is healthy ? Justify your answer. (La question 3 ne concerne pas le texte, elle s'adresse à vous).

III. Proposez un équivalent en anglais pour les cinq plats suivants (BEP 5 pts, CAP 10 pts) :

– avocat aux crevettes,

– côte de porc grillée aux herbes,

– sole beurre maître d'hôtel,

– pommes à l'anglaise,

– poire Belle-Hélène.

IV. Écrivez un court paragraphe (5 lignes environ) au prétérit sur votre stage de fin de première année BEP (quand a-t-il eu lieu ? où ? quelles ont été vos activités ? avez-vous apprécié cette période ? pourquoi ?) (BEP 5 pts).

Amiens

2

THÈME ABORDÉ | SPÉCIALITÉS
Services hôteliers | Hôtellerie-Restauration

WELCOME TO THE PATRAS HOTEL

Chef of the year

1. Gordon Ramsay, the chef de partie at the Guy Savoy restaurant in Paris, was the winner of the 1992 National Chef of the Year competition.

2. During the three-hour practical final yesterday morning, he cooked a four-course, four person menu which comprised :

3. lobster ravioli with ginger, velouté of asparagus ; roasted veal sweetbreads topped with creamed parsley ; and vanilla crème brûlée with two chocolates.

4. Ramsay was praised[1] by the judges for his calm throughout[2] the three-hour competition, as well as for the quality of the dishes produced at the end.

5. « I decided to treat the event as though[3] I was cooking a meal for four VIP[4] guests at Guy Savoy, and to forget that I was in a competition » explained Mr Ramsay.

Source : Caterer and Hotel Keeper. January 1992 (adapted).

QUESTIONS

I. Traduisez en français la totalité du texte « Chef of the Year » (BEP et CAP, 8 pts).

1. *to praise :* féliciter. 2. *throughout :* d'un bout à l'autre de... 3. *as though :* comme si. 4. *VIP :* Very Important Person.

II. En anglais, expliquez en une ou deux phrases les 11 services offerts par l'hôtel Patras. Numérotez vos réponses en anglais de 1 à 11 en respectant l'ordre du document (BEP et CAP, 12 pts).

(2 phrases au minimum par réponse pour la notation BEP, 1 phrase au minimum pour la notation CAP.)

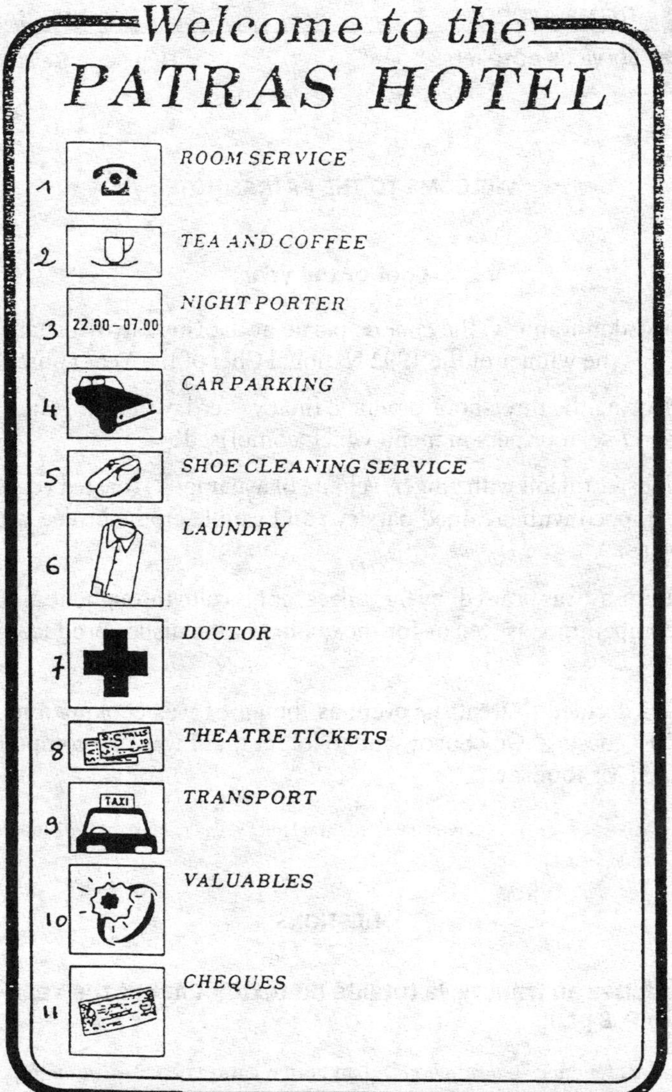

Bordeaux

3

THÈME — Confort/Équipement

SPÉCIALITÉ — Hôtellerie

A GUEST IS A GUEST

QUESTIONS

Voir document pp. 24-25.

I. Question à choix multiple. Cochez la bonne réponse (CAP 4 pts, BEP 4 pts) :

1. Giving the best to guests means :

a) offering facilities such as cable TV, telephone, mini-bar, chocolate or perfume.
b) offering more than cable TV, telephone, mini-bar, chocolate or perfume.
c) offering not just cable TV but also telephone, mini-bar, chocolate or perfume.

2. All over the world guests appreciate :

a) vacation and tourism with the Number 1 hotel.
b) safety and convenience with the Number 1 safe.
c) business and travels with the Number 1 attache-case.

3. The Elsafe is :

a) a personal safe.
b) an electronic mini-bar.
c) a personal computer.

4. Guests can use the Elsafe :

a) every day, at the reception desk of the hotel.
b) at any time, at either the reception desk of the hotel or in the privacy of their rooms.
c) at any time, in the privacy of their room.

II. Répondez en anglais (CAP 8 pts, BEP 4 pts) :

1. Write « 180.000 hotel rooms » : ....

2. In which European countries is the Elsafe available ? ....

A GUEST IS A GUEST, IS A GUEST, IS A GUEST ...
SAFE DEPOSIT

IN "THE ELSAFE HOTEL" A GUEST IS THE GUEST

3. Where are the people in picture 1 ? ....

4. What is the man doing in picture 2 ? ....

III. Cochez la bonne réponse (CAP 2 pts, BEP 1 pt) et justifiez votre choix en anglais (CAP 4 pts, BEP 3 pts) :

What sort of document is this ?

– a lesson on bank accounts,
– a page from a novel,
– an advertisement,
– a notice for use.

Justify (minimum 3 lines).

IV. De quoi s'agit-il ? Choisissez pour cette illustration le terme qui convient et justifiez votre choix d'une phrase en anglais (CAP 2 pts, BEP 2 pts) :

– a fridge
– a wardrobe
– a cupboard
– a clock
– a mini-bar
– a safe

Justify : ....
....
....
....
....

V. BEP seulement (6 pts) :

Vous êtes réceptionniste dans un hôtel. Vous recevez un couple de clients qui désirent faire une réservation. Rédigez le dialogue de votre conversation (10 lignes).

Pensez à accueillir vos clients, posez des questions polies. Vous pouvez utiliser le vocabulaire suivant : *name, nationality, home address, passport, registration card, reservation, room number, charge, date of departure, including breakfast, luggage, porter, to book, to check in/out*

Caen

4

THÈME ABORDÉ — Menu de restaurant

SPÉCIALITÉS — Hôtellerie/Restauration/Hébergement

LA REINE MATHILDE RESTAURANT

Mr et Mrs Smith have decided to celebrate their 20th wedding anniversary at La Reine Mathilde Restaurant in Caen.

Here is the menu :

A. ENTRÉES ET SALADES

Crème Dubarry	£ 3.00
Soupe à l'oignon gratinée	£ 2.95
Salade niçoise	£ 5.95
Quiche lorraine	£ 3.55
Salade du pêcheur	£ 3.25
Crudités	£ 1.95
Pizza des quatre saisons	£ 4.25
Bouchée à la reine	£ 5.75

B. POISSONS ET FRUITS DE MER

Sole grillée	£ 8.25
Sole meunière	£ 8.25
Truite aux amandes	£ 4.75
Homard mayonnaise	£ 11.90
Moules marinière	£ 4.00

C. VIANDES

Tournedos Rossini	£ 9.25
Escalope de veau à la normande	£ 6.50
Canard à l'orange	£ 7.50
Carré d'agneau	£ 6.15

D. **GARNITURES DE LÉGUMES AU CHOIX**

Pommes duchesse
Riz créole
Petits pois
Haricots verts
Frites

Plateau de fromages .... £ 3.50

E. **DESSERTS**

Crème caramel .... £ 2.25
Charlotte aux pommes .... £ 3.20
Tarte aux abricots .... £ 2.80
Salade de fruits frais .... £ 3.00
Crêpes suzette .... £ 2.95
Glaces et sorbets .... £ 1.95

F. **BOISSONS**

Cuvée du patron en carafe (rouge ou blanc)
0,25 l .... £ 2.20
0,50 l .... £ 3.50

Vins blancs
Muscadet-sur-lie .... £ 6.00
Riesling .... £ 8.00
Sancerre .... £ 9.25

Vins rouges
Saint-émilion .... £ 11.50
Châteauneuf-du-pape .... £ 15.00
Chinon .... £ 8.00

Rosés
Côtes-de-provence .... £ 5.50
Cabernet .... £ 6.75

Champagnes
Pommery .... £ 35.00
Canard-Duchesne .... £ 30.00

Cafés

Expresso	£ 1.20
Décaféiné	£ 1.40
Choix de thés	£ 1.80

All prices include VAT (18.6 %)
A service charge of 10 % will be added.

QUESTIONS

I. After reading the menu, you will explain five different dishes. Choose (BEP 10 pts, CAP 15 pts) :

1 from A (entrées et salades),

1 from B (poissons et fruits de mer),

1 from C (viandes),

1 from D (garniture de légumes au choix),

1 from E (desserts).

II. Mr and Mrs Smith have about the same taste and they have ordered the same menu except for the desserts :

– salade du pêcheur,
– sole meunière,
– canard à l'orange,
– cheese.

Mrs Smith has ordered a charlotte aux pommes and Mr Smith a salade de fruits frais.

a) Mr Smith has suggested a muscadet-sur-lie with the canard à l'orange.

What do you think of his choice (BEP 3 pts, CAP 2 pts) ?

b) What else would you suggest and why (BEP 4 pts, CAP 2 pts) ?

III. How much will they have to pay considering they will also have 2 coffees (2 expresso) (BEP 3 pts, CAP 1 pt) ?

Corse

5

THÈME ABORDÉ | SPÉCIALITÉS

Les vins | Hôtellerie/Restauration

→ **CORRIGÉ**

WINE DISTRICTS

In Portugal, Oporto is the centre of the wine area. Dão is the name of the district south of Oporto and port wine comes from the area north of the town. In Spain, the most famous wine, sherry, comes from the extreme south. But there are lighter Spanish wines, too. The best of these lighter table wines come from Rioja, north of Madrid. In France, the Champagne district produces the most famous sparkling wine. That's east of Paris. South of Paris, and running west to Nantes, is the Loire Valley which produces wines like Muscadet and Sancerre. The Bordeaux region is in the south-west of France. This area produces Médoc, St-Émilion, and Graves, for example. Just north of Lyon is the Burgundy wine district, the home of Beaujolais, Mâcon, and many others. In Italy, the most famous wine, Chianti, comes from the area south of Florence. The district to the east of Rome produces a famous white wine, Frascati.

QUESTIONS

I. Right or wrong ? Justify your answer (BEP 5 pts, CAP 10 pts) :

1. Sherry is a Portuguese wine.
2. Sancerre is produced in the Loire Valley.
3. Oporto is a famous red wine.
4. The Burgundy wine district is situated in England.
5. Spain only produces sherry.

II. Put the following sentences in the interrogative form (BEP et CAP 5 pts) :

1. Peter goes to the restaurant every sunday.

2. You are eating potatoes.
3. They drank a pint of beer in a pub.
4. I won't go to the cinema with you.
5. He would like to order an apple-pie.

III. Choose the right answer (CAP seulement, 5 pts) :

1. In august I .... to Paris
(go – went – gone – did).
2. My father told me that .... some apples on the table
(there were – there was – they were – they was).
3. I have bought .... different dresses
(for – four – woor – thour).
4. I want .... drink a glass of wine
(for – by – to – from).
5. Tomorrow, we .... buy a carpet
(did – have – not – will).

IV. Put the verbs into the correct tense (the simple present or the present continuous) (uniquement pour les candidats au BEP, 5 pts) :

1. My mother always (to make) a cake for my birthday.
2. He can't come now. He (to do) his homework.
3. He (to watch) all the football matches on television.
4. (You to go) to school already ?
5. Come and listen to the radio. The president (to speak).

V. Each of these sentences is the answer to a question. Write the questions (uniquement les candidats au BEP, 5 pts) :

1. I saw my bank manager.
2. They ate four.
3. I met her in Russia.
4. He arrived at half past eight.
5. Yes he did.

Lyon

6

THÈME ABORDÉ SPÉCIALITÉS

Garçon de café — Hôtellerie/Restauration

→ **CORRIGÉ**

THE HARD ROCK CAFÉ

SAVE THE PLANET

HARD ROCK CAFÉ

Menu

The café chef salad	£ 6.95
Bar-B-Que chicken	£ 8.95
Cheeseburger	£ 6.50
Linda McCartney's Veggie burger	£ 5.95
Hot fudge brownie	£ 3.50

The first restaurant in the chain opened in London in 1971. Now there are more than twenty Hard Rocks in the world.

Why are the cafés so popular ? Good American food, loud rock music, famous objects on the walls, and famous customers at the tables. You often have to queue to get in, but rock fans are happy to wait two hours or more to eat next to Peter Gabriel's guitar or Prince's purple jacket. The hard Rock café in Orlando Florida is the most successful restaurant in the world ; it serves 5,000 customers a day !

For Americans it is a great place to eat and perhaps see a star or two : Bruce Springsteen, Tina Turner, Phil Collins and Jim Courier are regular customers. For other people, it is like visiting America for the price of a meal.

The owners of the Hard Rock café want to do more than just feed the planet, they want to protect it. They write menus on recycled paper and they help campaigns for the protection of the environment. For example, they took tuna fish off the menu when environmentalists called for a tuna boycott.

All the Hard Rocks are very busy so the waitresses and waiters work hard. Lulu Sinnott works in the Hark Rock café in New York. She recently participated in some tests and discovered that she walks 20-24 km in a working day, carrying 9-13 kilos of plates and food !

QUESTIONS

I. Right/wrong. When wrong, justify your choice using information from the text (BEP 2,5 pts, CAP 5 pts) :

1. You never have to wait to eat in a Hard Rock Café.
2. You can meet famous stars there.
3. The Hard Rock Café in Orlando is less popular than other restaurants.
4. The owners don't care about environment.
5. A waitress must walk many kilometers every working day.

II. Make sentences with the following groups of words (BEP 2,5 pts, CAP 5 pts) :

1. reserve/ can/ a table/ I/ lunch/ for/ ?
2. 20 pounds/ the cost/ for/ is/ this menu
3. no/left : there is/ butter/ sorry
4. have/ a piece of/ I/ please/ Cheddar/ will
5. pepper/ on/ there is/ the table/ no/ left

III. Poser les questions correspondant à la partie soulignée des phrases suivantes (BEP et CAP, 5 pts) :

1. You spend <u>50 pounds</u> every month in restaurants.
2. We finish our season <u>at the end of september</u>.
3. The restaurant closes in winter, <u>because there are no customers</u>.
4. I have been cooking <u>since 9 o'clock this morning</u>.
5. The chef's speciality is <u>lamb loin with mint sauce</u>.

IV. Dialogue (BEP et CAP, 5 pts) (3 répliques minimum pour le serveur) :

Look at the Hard Rock café menu and imagine a dialogue between a waiter (or a waitress) and a customer.

V. Essay (BEP seulement, 5 pts) (3 raisons minimum) :

Would you like to work in a Hard Rock café ? Give your reasons.

Orléans-Tours

7

THÈME ABORDÉ — SPÉCIALITÉS

Serveur de restaurant

Hôtellerie/Restauration (BEP)
Restauration/Hébergement intégrés (CAP)

→ **CORRIGÉ**

AT THE RESTAURANT

« Hey ! What about the steak I ordered 40 minutes ago ? »

QUESTIONS

I. Regardez l'illustration et répondez aux questions suivantes en rédigeant des phrases complètes (BEP et CAP, 4 pts) :

1. Who is the man on the right ?

....

Describe his position :

....

2. Who is the man on the left ?

....

Describe his position :

....

II. Le client se plaint :
« Hey, what about the steak I ordered 40 minutes ago ? »

Imaginez deux répliques possibles du serveur (BEP 4 pts, CAP 2 pts) :

1. ....
....

2. ....
....

III. Pour chaque objet numéroté (sauf les nos 7 et 9), rédigez une phrase pour le présenter en utilisant les tournures « There is/There are » (BEP 4 pts, CAP 8 pts) :

Exemple : 7 here is a menu.
9 there is a wine list.

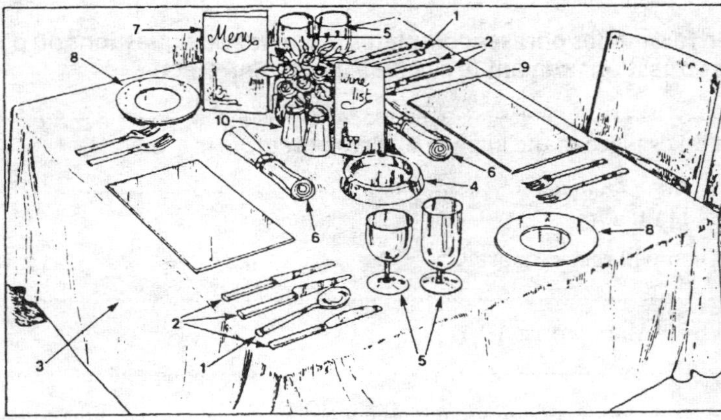

IV. Lisez le dialogue ci-dessous puis faites les exercices qui suivent :

The scene takes place in the kitchen of a restaurant. It is 11.30 a.m.

Jim : Hurry up, service will start in 30 minutes.

Tom : All right, all right, we're almost ready.

Mary (from the dining-room) : Do you think we'll have enough bread ? Maybe we should call the baker. We had more customers than usual for breakfast. It's because of the Wine and Food Festival.

Jim : Yes, it seems to be very successful this year. People are getting tired of diets and light food. They are going back to traditions. That's why I think today's main course, *Irish Stew will...*

Tom : Hey, you two, you told me to hurry up but you've been talking for 5 minutes.

Jim : OK, I'm coming.

Tom : Can you check the *seasoning* of the vegetable soup ?

Jim : It's perfect. You've really *improved* since you've been working with me.

Tom : Very funny indeed. Let me remind you that I graduated from an excellent *Hotel and Catering School.*

Mary (from the dining-room) : Hush boys, the first guests are arriving.

A) En faisant des phrases complètes répondez aux questions ou posez les questions suivant le cas (BEP 20 pts, CAP 5 pts) :

1. .... ?
It takes place in the kitchen of a restaurant.

2. .... ?
It's 11.30 a.m.

3. When will service start ?
....

4. Why is Mary worried ?
....

5. .... ?
He sells bread.

6. Why did they have more customers than usual ?
....

7. .... ?
It's the first meal of the day.

8. What are people getting tired of ?
.... ?

9. .... ?
He's been talking for 5 minutes.

10. .... ?
It's perfect.

B) En vous aidant du contexte, rayez les mauvaises réponses (a, b et c) (BEP et CAP, 4 pts) :

1. Dites si *Irish Stew* est :
une soupe / un plat de viande / un dessert / un hors-d'œuvre
Réponse : ....

2. Choisissez la traduction de *seasoning* :
saisonnier / assaisonnement / de saison / cuisson
Réponse : ....

3. Choisissez la traduction de *improved* :
progressé / régressé / improvisé / approuvé
Réponse : ....

4. Trouvez la traduction de *Hotel and Catering School* :
Réponse : ....

V. Faites correspondre les noms des plats à la description qui convient (BEP et CAP, 5 pts) :

1. Œufs mollets florentine ....
2. Œufs brouillés portugaise ....
3. Merlan en colère ....
4. Blanquette de veau à l'ancienne ....
5. Tournedos Rossini ....

a) Deep fried whiting
b) Soft boiled eggs with spinach and Mornay sauce
c) Veal stew with mushrooms and onions
d) Fillet steak served on a piece of toast and topped with a slice of foie gras
e) Scrambled eggs with tomato fondue

VII. Répondez aux questions concernant le dessin page suivante en faisant des phrases complètes (BEP 3 pts, CAP 6 pts) :

1. What's the man's job ? ....
2. Where is he working ? ....
3. What is he wearing ? ....
4. Name 4 ustensils he can use : ....

VI. Posez les questions correspondant aux réponses données (BEP seulement, 6 pts) :

1. .... ?
It's in the bucket on the side table.
2. .... ?
We have Camembert, Brie and Gruyère.
3. .... ?
You can pay cash, by cheque or by credit card.

VIII. Écrivez en anglais à quelles parties d'un menu correspondent les plats mentionnés ci-dessous (BEP et CAP, 4 pts) :

– .... Mixed salad
– .... Roast chicken with peas
– .... Cheddar and Stilton
– .... Apple pie

IX. Conjuguez le verbe entre parenthèses au temps qui convient (BEP 6 pts, CAP 2 pts) :

1. – We .... to the seaside last summer (to go).
– He .... tennis every Monday (to play).
– They .... the piano since the age of 5 (to learn).
– Look ! She .... the street (to cross).

SECRÉTARIAT/BUREAUTIQUE

Amiens

8

THÈME ABORDÉ | SPÉCIALITÉ

Matériel traditionnel | Secteur tertiaire

→ CORRIGÉ

SOUND IDEA

1. Ring Laura Newman at her office, and you can hear for yourself how business is booming : typewriters clatter[1] in the background, telephones constantly ring, and filing cabinets can be heard opening and shutting.

2. The business is real, but the sounds are fake[2] : Newman's background noises come from a tape recording.

3. The idea for an « office » tape[3] came to Newman after she set up her own business at her home in New York last year. Household noises in the background – the sound of her four young children, the family television – projected an unprofessional image to telephone callers.

4. Newman solved the problem by recording a collection of typical office noises. The result is a sound effects tape that worked so well that Newman has gone into business – selling it to other stay-at-home business people, at a price of $ 14.95.

5. Newman is now preparing a second tape with the sounds of computer printers and terminals. It is for people who want telephone callers to think they are surrounded by busy machines.

Source : Spotlight january 1989 (adapted).

QUESTIONS

I. Répondez en anglais aux questions suivantes, non par de simples mots mais par des phrases complètes (BEP 8 pts, CAP 10 pts) :

1. Does Laura work in a traditional office ?

2. Has Laura got any children ?

3. What could business people hear when they telephoned Laura ?

4. What did she do to project a good professional image on the phone ?

1. *to clatter :* faire du bruit. 2. *fake :* faux, truqué. 3. *a tape :* une banque magnétique.

5. How much does the sound effects tape cost ?

6. What people buy that sound effects tape ?

7. Working at home or working in an office ? What do you prefer ? Explain why.

II. En anglais, décrivez l'illustration en 4 à 5 lignes (BEP 6 pts, CAP 4 pts).

III. Traduisez en français les paragraphes 4 et 5 (de... ***Newman solved the problem...*** **à la fin du texte) (BEP et CAP, 6 pts).**

NB : Traduction : le passage à traduire est divisé en 5 phrases, indépendantes pour la notation. 1 point par phrase correctement traduite et 1 point pour la qualité d'ensemble de la traduction. Retrait de fraction(s) de points ou de point en fonction de la gravité des erreurs commises, jusqu'à concurrence de 1 point par phrase.

Lille

9

THÈME ABORDÉ | SPÉCIALITÉ

Ordinateurs | Secteur tertiaire

→ **CORRIGÉ**

A BYTE AT THE RESTAURANT

John Thomson at the Green Rooms

1. John Thomson and wife Gina always dreamt of owning and running a traditional English tea-room far from the noisy atmosphere of the school classrooms where they worked.

2. They found an old shop in Essex, which they converted into a restaurant, the Green Rooms. The restaurant was very successful, but there were problems, such as when a room full of customers asked for their bills[1] at the same time late in the evening.

3. The launch[2] of cheap computers gave Mr Thomson the idea of computerised billing. He bought a cheap model and an accounts package[3], but found the program very slow and thought he could do better himself.

4. He became interested in programming and, with no previous experience, wrote a billing program in about a month. « I was surprised at how interesting it was. When I gave up teaching, I never thought I would become a computer programmer » says Mr Thomson. Many customers were so impressed that they asked Mr Thomson to write tailor-made accounting programmes[4].

1. *the bill :* la facture, l'addition. 2. *to launch a new product :* lancer un nouveau produit. 3. *an accounts package :* un logiciel de comptabilité. 4. *an accounting programme :* un programme de comptabilité.

5. Business from programming is growing fast at about £ 80,000 a year / and the turnover[5] of the restaurant is approaching £ 130,000. / But there are no overheads[6], with the computing business, / and the restaurant is now becoming a sideline[7], only opening on friday and saturday evenings. / Mr Thomson is even considering converting the restaurant into a computer shop.

Source : The Daily Telegraph, october 26, 1992 (adapted).

QUESTIONS

I. Répondez en anglais aux questions suivantes, non par de simples mots mais par des phrases complètes (BEP 8 pts, CAP 10 pts) :

1. What was Mr and Mrs Thomson's job before opening The Green Rooms ?

2. Is The Green Rooms a computer shop ?

3. What was Mr Thomson's problem when his restaurant was full of customers ?

4. What did he do to make billing easier and quicker ?

5. Was he pleased with the accounts package ?

6. Did he decide to buy a new and better accounts package ?

7. Was Mr Thomson an expert computer programmer at the beginning ?

8. What is going to change in Mr Thomson's professional life ?

II. En anglais, décrivez l'illustration en 4 à 5 lignes (BEP 6 pts, CAP 4 pts).

III. Traduisez en français le paragraphe 5 (de *Business from programming...* à la fin du texte) (BEP et CAP, 6 pts).

NB : Le paragraphe à traduire est divisé en 5 unités indépendantes pour la notation, repérées par des barres obliques. 1 point par unité correctement traduite et 1 point pour la qualité d'ensemble de la traduction. Retrait de fraction(s) de point ou de point selon la gravité des erreurs commises, jusqu'à concurrence de 1 point par unité.

5. *the turnover :* le chiffre d'affaires. 6. *overheads :* les frais généraux. 7. *a sideline :* une activité secondaire.

Nice

10

THÈME ABORDÉ

Ordinateurs portables

SPÉCIALITÉS

CAS/ACC/ESAC

→ **CORRIGÉ**

TOSHIBA NOTEBOOKS

QUESTIONS

Les candidats au BEP traiteront toutes les questions.
Les candidats au CAP traiteront les questions I et II.

I. Regardez bien ce document, puis répondez aux questions suivantes en anglais (BEP 9 pts, CAP 16 pts) :

1. What product is advertised here ? (1 phrase) (BEP1 pt, CAP 2 pts)
2. Who is the advertiser ? (1 phrase) (BEP 1 pt, CAP 2 pts)
3. Describe one person, A B or C on the picture (age, appearance). Imagine... (3 phrases) (BEP 3 pts, CAP 6 pts)
4. What is his (or her) job ? Give 2 different possibilities. (BEP 2 pts, CAP 3 pts)
5. Give 2 qualities of the product after reading the text. (BEP 2 pts, CAP 3 pts)

II. Traduisez en vous aidant du texte (BEP 6 pts, CAP 4 pts) :

1. De plus en plus de gens utilisent les ordinateurs.
2. Avaient-ils la situation bien en main ?
3. Où qu'il aille, il n'oublie pas son ordinateur.
4. Compte-t-elle sur leur aide ?

III. Essai (BEP seulement, 5 pts) :

Do you like computers ? Give your reasons to be for or against (environ 45 mots).

Grenoble

11

THÈME ABORDÉ — SPÉCIALITÉ

Répondeurs téléphoniques — Secteur tertiaire

→ CORRIGÉ

TALKING TELEPHONES

Ten years ago people had one telephone in the house and one in the office. Today, people have telephones everywhere : in the house, in the car, in the garden. You even see people walking round the streets with cordless telephones.

Another new thing is the answerphone but nobody likes it. In fact callers have many problems about how to speak to it because it is very difficult to have a conversation with a machine. Answerphone owners have problems too, mainly because of the message they have to record.

If the time left for the message is too short, the caller doesn't have time to think, in that case he is discouraged and quickly puts down the receiver.

Nevertheless, life has become easier since the invention of the telephone and it will go on improving as technology itself improves : let's just see the French minitel's surprising success.

QUESTIONS

I. Répondez en anglais aux questions suivantes (4 pts) :

1. Where do people have telephones nowadays ? What about ten years ago ?
2. What is the advantage of an answerphone ?
3. Why does a caller have problems with the answerphone ?
   What about the owner ?
4. Why has life become easier since the invention of the telephone ?

II. Traduction. Traduisez le premier paragraphe (3 pts).

III. Posez la question portant sur les mots soulignés (2pts) :

1. <u>Ten years ago</u> people had one telephone in the house.
2. He quickly puts down <u>the receiver</u>.

IV. Transformez la structure verbale en fonction de l'indicateur de temps (2 pts) :

1. (Ten years ago) people had telephone in the house.

In the future ....

2. He quickly puts down the receiver.

If he was discouraged ....

V. Essay (5 pts) :

You phone your friend Mike to invite him to your birthday party but he is out. So you have to leave the message on his answerphone. What do you say ?

Write the message with all the following elements :

– you invite him to your party,

– you give the day and the time of the party,

– you'd like him to call you back to confirm so don't forget to leave your telephone number !

Corse

12

THÈME ABORDÉ

Activités de secrétariat

SPÉCIALITÉS

CAS/ACC/ESAC

→ **CORRIGÉ**

DEAR SIR

Dear Sir,

I often wonder what makes girls want to become secretaries when they leave school. I did, many years ago, and I made a terrible mistake. A secretary is never well-paid and sometimes secretaries spend so much time making tea and coffee and making telephone calls that they have very little time for typing.

I am quite lucky that my three bosses can make tea. But they can't answer the telephone because they are always too busy. And when they want to dictate a letter, it's urgent. If I have a lunch-appointment or a meeting after work somewhere, I still have to type their letters first. The person who's waiting for me gets tired and phones later to ask why I was not there. All I can do is to explain that I'm a secretary and that's what I'm there for– Bosses are allowed to get angry, secretaries aren't.

Perhaps one day I'll find a quieter, more relaxing job.

Yours faithfully,

Anne White.

QUESTIONS

I. Right or wrong ? Justify your answer when it is wrong (BEP et CAP, 5 pts)

1. Anne White likes her work as a secretary.

....

....

2. She thinks that a secretary doesn't earn much.

....

....

3. She has to spend all day typing.

....

....

4. She always leaves her office on time.

....

....

5. Anne White often gets angry with people.

....

....

II. Choose the correct word to complete each sentence (BEP et CAP, 5 pts) :

1. It's .... computer.

a) there, *b)* theirs, *c)* their, *d)* they're.

2. I look forward .... from you.

a) to hearing, *b)* hearing, *c)* hear, *d)* to hear.

3. Have you .... to London before ?

a) been, *b)* gone, *c)* go, *d)* went.

4. .... typewriter is that ?

a) his, *b)* who, *c)* whose, *d)* who's.

5. It's .... monday morning.

a) in, *b)* at, *c)* on, *d)* to.

III. Write the past participle of the verbs in these sentences (BEP et CAP, 3 pts) :

1. The desk was (break) : ....

2. I have not (send) the telex yet : ....

3. Have you (see) him before ? : ....

IV. Write the comparatives of the adjectives in these sentences (BEP et CAP, 3 pts) :

1. This photocopier is (easy) to use than that one.

2. John earns (little) money than Peter.

3. My boss is (intelligent) than you.

V. Put the following sentences into the interrogative form (CAP seulement, 4 pts) :

1. It's going to take a week.
2. They closed that factory last december.
3. She must leave early today.
4. She's got a new typewriter.

VI. Choose the right tense (BEP seulement, 4 pts) :

1. He always (to drive) to work.
2. At the moment they (to type).
3. I (not to go) to work yesterday.
4. I (can) take shorthand next year.

Nantes

13

THÈME ABORDÉ — SPÉCIALITÉS

Carte de client privilégié — Tertiaire/Alimentation/Hôtellerie

→ CORRIGÉ

HARRODS ACCOUNT CARD

A higher level of service for busy people

The real value of becoming an Account Cardholder at Harrods is the way it makes life easier. The busier you are, the more you will appreciate the difference the Harrods card makes.

For a start, there are the special Invitation Only Account Customer evenings. The famous Harrods catalogues will also start to appear on your door*mat*[1] before each Harrods Sale and every special promotion, not forgetting Christmas.

You simply pick out what you need and telephone in your order at your leisure[2] : Delivery is free within our central London van delivery area.

You'll find the sheer variety[3] at Harrods makes the store highly practical for everyday items as well.

Whether[4] you need a bottle of wine for unexpected guests[4], or you run out of cat food, or you're looking for the latest CD release, the chances are we've got just what you're after.

And an Account Card is the most convenient way to get it.

Every day, there's something you need at Harrods :

Most of us would prefer to receive a better standard of service when we shop – the sort of service you would expect at Harrods. Yet perhaps the store does not spring to mind[5] for « everyday » purchases[6].

In fact, the sheer variety on offer througho*ut*[7] literally dozens of different departments[8] makes Harrods the supremely practical store. Virtually every day, there's something you need here. We will send you a complete Guide to the store with your Account Card.

If you would like to become an Account Customer and open up the world of Harrods, complete the Application below and return it to us. We look forward to receiving your application[9].

1. le pas de la porte. 2. à votre guise/comme vous voulez. 3. (ici) une grande variété. 4. que (vous) ... ou bien que ... 5. venir à l'esprit. 6. achats. 7. réparti(e) sur. 8. rayons (d'un grand magasin). 9. formulaire.

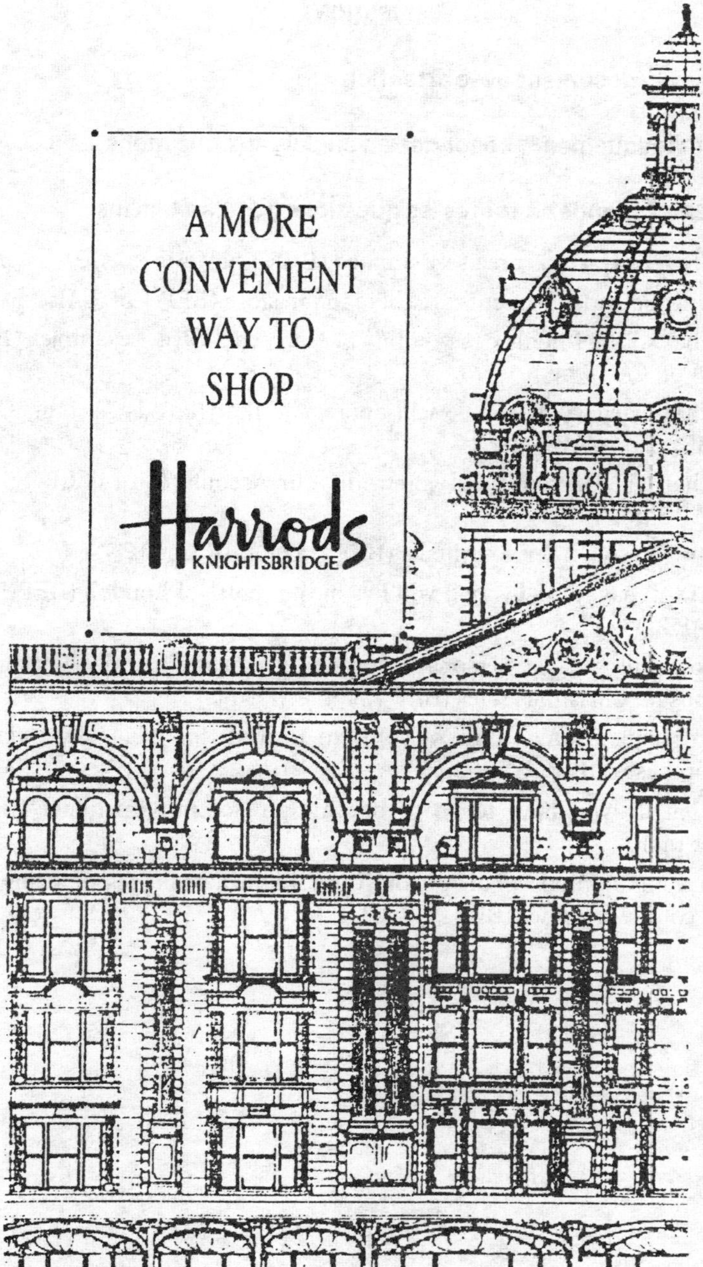
A MORE
CONVENIENT
WAY TO
SHOP
Harrods
KNIGHTSBRIDGE

QUESTIONS

I. Lisez le document avec attention.

II. CAP uniquement : Répondez en anglais aux questions 1 à 8.

III. BEP : Répondez à toutes les questions (nos 1 à 11 inclus).

1. Where is Harrods precisely situated (BEP 1 pt, CAP 2 pts) ?
2. How many departments are there in the store (BEP 1 pt, CAP 2 pts) ?
3. What sorts of items can you buy at Harrods ? Give 3 examples (BEP 1,5 pt, CAP 3 pts) ?
4. What category of people will appreciate the Harrods Account Card (BEP 1 pt, CAP 2 pts) ?
5. What will Harrods send you with your Account Card (BEP 1,5 pt, CAP 3 pts) ?
6. How do you order your items (BEP 1,5 pt, CAP 3 pts) ?
7. Do you pay for delivery if you live in the centre of London (BEP 1 pt, CAP 2 pts) ?
8. How will you get personal information concerning special promotions on Christmas sales (BEP 1,5 pt, CAP 3 pts) ?
9. Do people usually think of going to Harrods for their « everyday » purchases (BEP, 2,5 pts) ?
10. What do you have to do to become an Account Customer (BEP, 2,5 pts) ?
11. In your opinion, what are the three main advantages of being an Account Customer (BEP, 5 pts) ?

THÈMES GÉNÉRAUX

Poitiers

14

THÈME ABORDÉ — SPÉCIALITÉS

Argent de poche — CAS/ACC/ESAC

→ **CORRIGÉ**

BRITISH BANKS

Barclays, and other British banks have made it easier for 11 – to 16 – year – olds to have their own bank accounts and bank cards. But now, some parents are questioning how much financial independence they should allow their children.

Bill and Anne Freeman live in Ealing, a London suburb. Bill is a computer technician, Anne is a secretary. They have two children. Timothy, 16, and Wendy, 14. When Timothy found a part-time job[1] at a McDonald's restaurant, he and his parents were pleased. « We thought it was very good for him to earn his own money », said Anne. « It's extremely important for young people to understand that money doesn't grow on trees, and that we usually work quite hard to get it. Also, we thought Timothy would be happier if he didn't have to ask us for money all the time. »

The Freemans decided they would stop Timothy's pocket money but give him money if he really needed it. He promised to put part of his salary in the bank each week. This seemed to work well, but suddendly Bill and Anne have found themselves with a problem.

« Tim asked us to buy him an £80 pair of Chipie jeans », explains Bill. « I refused to buy the jeans because I thought the price was scandalous. Timothy considered the jeans a necessity. I saw it as a matter of principle. » Timothy's response was, « I'll buy the jeans with my own money », and he went straight[2] to the bank.

Bill and Anne have asked many questions. Is it right for their son to be able to buy something when it goes against their principles. Is it normal that he doesn't contribute financially at all to the family ? « We're worried that, perhaps, in giving our son more independence », said Anne, « we are in fact contributing to the destruction of important values. »

From *Easy Speakeasy,* march 1992.

1. *a part-time job :* you don't work all the time, only a few hours a week. 2. *straight :* (ici) directly.

QUESTIONS

I. Right or wrong ? (Justifiez vos réponses en citant le texte) (10 pts) :

1. Timothy is younger than his sister.
2. Timothy decided to sell « Chipie » jeans to earn his own money.
3. His parents were satisfied with his decision to have a part-time job.
4. Anne thinks it's important for young people to learn that money isn't easy to earn.
5. Timothy spends all the money he gets from his job.
6. Timothy is paid at the end of each month.
7. The problem was that Timothy wanted to buy an expensive pair of jeans.
8. Anne and Bill wonder if Timothy should buy things with his own money when they don't agree.
9. Timothy gives his parents a bit of his salary to help them pay for food, petrol, electricity, etc.
10. Timothy's parents think that having too much pocket money is not a good solution because young people then think it is very easy to buy what they want.

II. Posez des questions sur les éléments soulignés (4 pts) :

1. Bill and Anne live <u>in Ealing</u>.
2. They live <u>with their two children</u>.
3. Timothy is <u>16</u>.
4. timothy found <u>a part-time job</u>.
5. He's had this job <u>for 3 months</u>.
6. He'll put part of his salary in the bank <u>each week</u>.
7. His pair of jeans was <u>£80</u>.
8. The bank is <u>2 miles</u> from Timothy's house.

III. Essay / Talking about pocket money (40 to 60 words) (6 pts) :

Here are some questions to help you express yourself on this subject :

What do you think of Timothy's parents' reaction ? Do you think they are wrong ? Do *you* get pocket money ? Do you think it's normal and necessary ? What do you do with it ? Would you like a part-time job ? Why ? What sort of job ? How would you feel ? Etc.

Strasbourg

15

THÈME ABORDÉ — Désertification rurale

SPÉCIALITÉS — ACC/CAS/Distribution-Magasinage/ESAC

→ CORRIGÉ

THERE'S NOTHING TO KEEP YOUNGSTERS HERE

Dictionnaire non autorisé

On a lonely hill, high in the Pennines, the market town of Alston is struggling for survival.

Its problems are typical of those afflicting an increasing number of rural communities.

Once a prosperous mining centre with up to 10,000 inhabitants, the Cumbrian town now relies on[1] tourism and a handful of small businesses to keep it alive. Its population is below 2,000, and falling.

Lifelong resident Sandra Elliott, 46, said : « Many of the young people have moved away because there's nothing for them to stay for. A lot of old and retired people have moved in, and many of them have second homes or holiday homes. »

Alston, set on a hillside at 1,000 ft, was once described as « Britain's highest market town ». But there is no longer a market. A post office, supermarket, two grocery shops, newsagent's and two schools still cling to[2] its steep cobbled streets[3]. But the butcher's went into liquidation last week.

Until 1980, an iron foundry provided jobs for nearly a third of the town's workers. When it closed the unemployment rate shot up to 37 per cent and even now is 12.5 per cent, just above the national average[4].

Since the closure, the local council has tried to encourage diversification. The town now has two engineering companies, a firm manufacturing waterproof clothing and a building concern.

Tourism is fortunately flourishing, and agriculture has long been a vital source of income. But with upland farming no longer viable in many cases, the rural side of life is threatened.

Alston also suffers from its remote[5] position. The nearest town of any size, Penrith, is 20 miles away. There are no trains, and the bus service is extremely limited. As a result, locals say, the winter months can be very quiet and depressing.

Daily Mail, thursday, september 10 1992.

1. *to rely on :* reposer sur. 2. *to cling to :* s'accrocher à. 3. *steep cobbled streets :* rues pavées escarpées. 4. *average :* moyenne. 5. *remote :* isolé.

QUESTIONS

I. Juste ou faux ? Si l'élément souligné est faux, rayez-le et notez la bonne réponse en dessous, telle qu'elle figure dans le texte (BEP 3,5 pts, CAP 7 pts) :

1. Alston is in Great Britain.

....

2. Alston is a market town in the plain.

....

3. The population of Alston is going up.

....

4. The unemployment rate is now thirty-seven percent.

....

5. Tourism is not successful.

....

6. Many young people live in Alston.

....

7. Alston was a rich mining center.

....

II. Find in the text three reasons why young people leave the town of Alston (BEP seulement, 3 pts) :

1. ....

....

2. ....

....

3. ....

....

III. À partir des informations contenues dans le texte, complétez les phrases suivantes avec les mots ci-dessous (BEP et CAP, 2,5 pts) :

no – much – many – a lot of – a few

There aren't .... young people in Alston because there isn't .... to do in this town. .... old people live there. The means of transportation are limited as there are .... trains and only .... buses every day.

IV. Posez la question pour laquelle l'élément souligné est la réponse (BEP et CAP, 4 pts) :

1. Many young people leave <u>because of unemployment</u>.

....

2. The butcher's shop went into liquidation <u>last week</u>.

....

3. The town now has <u>two</u> engineering companies.

....

4. Penrith is <u>20 miles away</u>.

....

V. Trouvez dans le texte les phrases dont le sens est équivalent aux phrases suivantes (BEP et CAP, 3 pts) :

1. Alston is fighting for life :

....

2. The number of the unemployed went up to a high percentage :

....

3. Alston is the victim of its geographical situation too :

....

VI. Répondez en anglais
– en six lignes minimum pour le BEP (4 pts),
– en quatre lignes minimum pour le CAP (3,5 pts) :

Would you prefer to live in a city or in the country ? Say why.

Polynésie française

16

THÈME ABORDÉ — SPÉCIALITÉS

Absentéisme dans l'entreprise — Tous BEP/CAP rénovés

→ CORRIGÉ

KEEPING THE WORKERS AT WORK

An Australian Company « Goodyear » is prepared to give away colour TV sets, fur coats, diamond rings and a chance to win 12,000 Australian dollars in ready cash to its employees. The only point is that they have to come to work regularly.

Absenteism is a problem throughout Australian industry. It seems to be caused by different factors : the wonderful climate, the sick days[1] Australians are entitled to[2] take, job boredom[3], monotony from the assembly line work.

So, Goodyear began a campaign against absenteism. First, there was a hand-delivered letter to all the employees explaining that if they didn't miss a day for any reason at all they would qualify to win one of the prizes. Then, other procedures such a nicer, brightly painted surroundings and piped music[4] have been tried. The company is also considering putting on lunchtime concerts to keep people's mids off their work.

(Adapted from the *Financial Times*.)

QUESTIONS

I. Compréhension. Choose the right answer (BEP 4 pts, CAP 8 pts) :

1. For the Australian Company « Goodyear », the main problem is :

a) the assembly line work,
b) boredom,
c) absenteism.

2. In Australia people will be given prizes if :

a) they go to work when the weather is fine,
b) they don't miss a day for any reason at all,
c) they occasionally go to work.

1. *sick days :* congé de maladie. 2. *to be entitled to :* avoir le droit de. 3. *boredom :* ennui. 4. *piped music :* musique d'ambiance.

3. If they come to work regularly people will win :

a) 12 000 Australian dollars in cheque,
b) one extra week holiday,
c) 12 000 Australian dollars in ready cash.

4. The company has tried :

a) to paint the buildings in dark colour,
b) to have piped music throughout the factory,
c) to organize sports every day.

II. Grammar. Find the questions corresponding to these answers (BEP et CAP, 4 pts) :

1. Absenteism is the big problem for Goodyear.
2. Goodyear began a campaign against absenteism.
3. They may get some prizes when they work regularly.
4. Concerts will make people happy at work.

III. Translation

1. Translate into French (BEP et CAP, 2 pts) :

There was a hand-delivered letter to all the employees explaining that if they didn't miss a day for any reason at all, they would win a prize.

2. Translate into English (BEP 4 pts et CAP 2 pts) :

L'absentéisme semble être provoqué par différents facteurs.

Les bons ouvriers auront droit à un prix s'ils viennent travailler régulièrement.

IV. Rédaction en anglais (8 à 10 lignes). Why is absenteism a real problem for a company (BEP 6 pts, CAP 4 pts) ?

– influence on the production,

– problems for the worker.

Suggest different ways to create better working conditions :

– buildings / surroundings,

– timetable / free time,

– sports and other group activities,

– etc.

Orléans-Tours

17

THÈME ABORDÉ — SPÉCIALITÉS

Travail saisonnier — CAS/ACC/Distribution-Magasinage/ESAC

→ CORRIGÉ

WORKING HOLIDAYS

When it's time to choose a holiday, you suddenly notice one of the most important differences between young people and their parents : young people haven't got much money. So often, the only sort of holiday they can afford[1] is a working holiday.

There's unemployment everywhere in Europe now. So the only sort of work that's still reasonably easy to find is seasonal work. There are two main sorts. One is fruit-picking, especially grapes[2]. The other is tourism-hotels, restaurants, holiday camps. Fortunately, both sorts tend to be in nice, sunny places !

Obviously, the safest thing to do is to find a job before you leave home. This used to be difficult. But now four or five guides to holiday jobs are published every year. Your local bookshop will have them. Go and look ! Even if you don't get a job from them, you'll get lots of useful information especially about what sort of fruit is picked where and when. You'll feel a bit silly if you go to the South of France to pick cherries[3] in August and find the last cherry was picked two months ago.

If these guides don't work for you, there are two other ways to find a job. First, ask your friends if they've had any good summer jobs or if they know anything about the places which might have jobs and write to all the possible employers, mentioning your friends. This often works. Second, if you can't find a job before you go, you can go anyway and look when you get there. Find out before you go where the jobs are. Be prepared to spend several days looking hard, going to see employers and being told to go away. Above all, if you can't get a job and you have only enough money left to come home, then come home ! It's hard ! But it can be worth it[4].

Whatever[5] you do, rule[6] number one is this : always find out as much as you can before you go from other people and from books. And be prepared ! Some farmers don't give you anywhere to live, you will probably need a sleeping-bag and perhaps a tent, too.

1. *to afford :* pouvoir s'offrir. 2. *grapes :* raisin. 3. *cherries :* cerises. 4. *to be worth it :* en valoir la peine. 5. *whatever :* quoique. 6. *rule :* règle.

QUESTIONS

I. Compréhension :

1. Parmi les trois titres suivants, lequel pourrait convenir au texte ? Cochez la réponse correcte (BEP 0,5 pt, CAP 1 pt) :

- Tourism for workers ❑
- Working holiday in Europe ❑
- Holiday abroad ❑

2. Relevez dans le texte les expressions correspondant aux définitions ci-dessous (BEP 2,5 pts, CAP 5 pts) :

a) The problem of not having a job.

....

b) People who pick fruit.

....

c) What you usually use at night when you're in a tent.

....

d) Where you can buy newspapers.

....

e) Jobs you do in July and August.

....

3. Dites si les affirmations sont exactes (right) ou fausses (wrong), et justifiez par des expressions tirées du texte dans les deux cas (BEP et CAP, 5 pts) :

a) Many young people have got enough money to spend their holiday.

....

b) They find it more and more difficult to find summer jobs in Europe.

....

c) Only one guide has been published.

....

d) There aren't any other ways for young people to get jobs abroad.

....

e) They generally work in fruit-picking or in tourism.

....

f) Cherries can be picked in August in France.

....

g) Young people can always sleep at the farm.

....

h) It's difficult to find a job.

....

i) They'd better go home if they can't find a job.

....

j) It doesn't matter if they don't get any information before leaving.

....

II. Compétence linguistique :

1. Posez la question correspondant à l'élément souligné de la phrase (BEP 5 pts ; CAP, a, b, c seulement, 6 pts) :

a) Guides are published every year.

....

b) They know about places of work.

....

c) They found jobs in farms.

....

d) She'll go with her friend.

....

e) He has left his car home.

....

2. Relevez deux superlatifs dans le texte (BEP et CAP), puis traduisez-les (BEP seulement) (BEP 2 pts, CAP 1 pt) :

a) .... = ...

b) .... = ...

3. Conjuguez les verbes au temps qui convient après avoir observé les repères de temps (BEP 3 pts ; CAP, b, c seulement, 2 pts) :

a) They (buy) a new guide last week.

....

b) He (pick) fruit next summer.

....

c) He (go) to France every summer.

....

III. Production (60 mots) (BEP seulement, 2 pts) :

- Would you go and work in a foreign country, in Europe ? Where would you go ? How long would you stay ? What would you do ?

Caen

18

THÈME ABORDÉ | SPÉCIALITÉS

Aide humanitaire | CAS/ACC/ESAC + Arts de la dentelle

→ CORRIGÉ

A FRENCH DOCTOR IN ENGLISH-SPEAKING AFRICA

Geneviève Begkoyian has been with Médecins sans Frontières since 1989, working, until recently, in refugee camps in South Africa and Malawi.

Today : *How did you become involved in humanitarian work ?*

Geneviève Begkoyian : I was an intern in a hospital in Quimper when a doctor friend asked me to participate in the emergency[1] aid mission « SOS Arménie », in order to help the victims of the 1989 earthquake[2] there. I spent five weeks in Armenia, and learned how important an outstretched[3] hand and a bit of human warmth could be in medical emergencies. I returned to France to finish my thesis, and immediately volunteered[4] for a mission with Médecins sans Frontières in South Africa, then eight months later in Malawi.

What did your work in those two countries involve ?

I took care of the many people who had fled[5] the massacres and brutalities of the civil war in nearby[6] Mozambique. My main task in the refugee camps was simply to help these people survive by providing nourishment, clean water and by giving vaccinations to the children.

How did you communicate ?

With the nurses and doctors from Malawi and South Africa we spoke English. In South Africa, though, the blacks taught us to speak Zulu, and in Malawi they taught us the Chichewa dialect spoken there and in Mozambique. In both countries we developed very strong ties[7] of friendship with the local population. It made it very hard for me to leave these camps.

1. *emergency :* urgence. 2. *earthquake :* tremblement de terre. 3. *outstretched :* tendue. 4. *to volunteer :* se porter volontaire. 5. *to flee :* fuir. 6. *nearby :* proche. 7. *ties :* liens.

What is your fondest memory of your experiences abroad ?

The day Nelson Mandela was liberated. I was in a black homeland in South Africa at the time. As soon as we heard the news, the other MSF workers and I ran out in the streets to join the blacks ; we celebrated with them all night long ! for them, we were living proof[8] that whites could be as overjoyed[9] as blacks about the hopes for a new South Africa.

And your worst memory ?

The death of a child in Malawi. Another doctor and I had taken an extra 15 minutes to talk and relax a bit before continuing our rounds[10]. When we entered the tent for cholera victims, we found a one-year-old whom we hadn't seen before. It was obvious that he was in a critical condition, and a few minutes later he died in our arms. I couldn't stop thinking thaf if I hadn't taken those extra 15 minutes, we might have been able to save him.

When you return to France you always do a lot of public relations work.

Yes. It's extremely important that people should be informed about human suffering[11] around the world. If you write about the problems of Africa in your magazine, I feel that part of the battle has already been won.

Interview by Barbara Oudiz.

8. *proof :* preuve. 9. *overjoyed :* au comble de la joie. 10. *rounds :* visites. 11. *suffering :* souffrance.

QUESTIONS

Could you please answer the following questions.

I. Comprehension (BEP et CAP, 10 pts) :

1. Who is Geneviève Begkoyian ?

2. Why did she decide to spend five weeks in Armenia ?

3. What did she do in Africa ?

4. Which languages did she use while she was in Africa ?

II. Reporting her experience (BEP et CAP, 5 pts) :

1. What is her best memory ?

2. What is her worst memory ?

III. Personal expression (traiter un sujet au choix) (BEP seulement, 5 pts) :

1. Do you think it is important to be informed about human suffering around the world ?

ou

2. Would you like to work in a foreign country ? Say why ?

III. Traduire en français (CAP seulement, 5 pts) le premier paragraphe de :

« I was a intern... » jusqu'à « eight months later in Malawi ».

Lyon

19

THÈME ABORDÉ
Vedettariat

SPÉCIALITÉS
BEP/CAP tertiaires

→ CORRIGÉ

« AIR » JORDAN

Air Jordan is not the name of an airline company, it is basketball star Michael Jordan's nickname.

Why ? Because he jumps so high that people say he spends more time in the air than on the ground. He is a fabulous basketball player and he has helped his team, the Chicago Bulls, win the last two championships. He himself has been chosen MVP (Most Valuable Player) in the National League three times, and he won his second Olympic gold medal in Barcelona this summer.

So what could he be unhappy about ? His success ! Michael sometimes thinks he is *too* successful. He is almost a prisoner of his **fame.** Like Michael Jackson or Madonna, he cannot walk down the street without attracting a crowd. When he goes to the movies he comes late and leaves early so the other spectators won't see him. That's no fun ! In Barcelona this summer, Michael and the other players on the Dream Team stayed in a hotel to escape the crowds at the Olympic village.

Once, when the Bulls were playing a game in Canada, Michael went to a restaurant and a discotheque after the game. Nobody recognized him, and he had a great time. But at home in the USA he could never do that. That's why he likes to wear disguises. But he is so tall that people often recognize him anyway.

Even if it sometimes makes his life difficult, Michael is proud of his success. He worked hard to become a basketball player and he still works hard to be the best.

Easy Speakeasy, nov.-déc. 92.

QUESTIONS

Les candidats au BEP traitent les 3 questions.
Les candidats au CAP traitent les questions I et II.

I. Imagine you are a reporter interviewing Michael Jordan. Ask him 10 questions about the following items (BEP et CAP, 10 pts) :

1. name
2. nickname
3. date of birth
4. place of birth
5. nationality
6. height
7. occupation
8. team
9. uniform number
10. letters received

Write down Michael's answers using his CV

Michael's CV

Name	:	Michael Jeffrey Jordan
Nickname	:	Air Jordan
Birth	:	February 17, 1963 New York-USA
Height	:	6 feet 6 inches
Team	:	Chicago Bulls
Uniform number : 23		
Fan mail	:	23,000 letters a month

II. Answer the questions (BEP 4 pts, CAP 10 pts) :

1. How can Michael Jordan's nickname be justified ?
2. What is he unhappy about ?
3. What are the problems of being so successful ? Give examples.
4. Why does Michael wear disguises ? Is it really efficient ?

III. Essay (BEP seulement, 6 pts) :

Would you like to be famous ?
Why or why not ?

Rennes

20

THÈME ABORDÉ — Vedettariat (précoce)

SPÉCIALITÉS — Secteur tertiaire

THIS BOY IS JUST FOUR, BUT ALREADY HE'S NUMBER ONE IN THE POP CHARTS

from Peter Shard

He is, in fact, just four years old and has been living with the sound of music since before he was born.

During his final seven months in the womb[1], pop and rap filled his parents' Paris apartment. And by the age of two, Jordy was in tune with the rhythms, beating a spoon on a plate in time to the sounds that came over the radio.

Then one day, aged just three, he wandered[2] into his father's home studio and picked up a microphone. The result was a cassette, a bit of Christmas run strictly for family consumption[3].

In the past month, his single has sold 200,000 copies, and for the past two weeks has been proudly at the top of the French charts. In November the English version of this admittedly rather monotonous song will hit the shops here – just in time for the Christmas market.

Of course, the cynics accuse his parents, record producer Claude Lemoine and his wife Patricia, a radio announcer, of exploiting the child for their own ends[4]. It is a charge his mother strongly denies. « He is singing about issues that matter[5] to four-year-olds », she insists, rather unconvincingly.

But she could be right. One verse runs : « Wake up kids and yell at your mum/don't let her leave you all on your own/stuck in front of boring TV/while she spends hours on the phone. »

Already Jordy talks of a singing career. « One day I want a Harley Davidson, just like Johnny », he says.

The Lemoines were certainly not prepared for the success that was to follow. Now their task is to ensure that it doesn't go to his head.

« We want him to have a normal life, a normal education and to make sure this success doesn't harm[6] him for life », Patricia says.

1. *womb :* ventre. 2. *to wander :* s'aventurer. 3. *consumption :* consommation. 4. *for their own ends :* pour leur profit personnel. 5. *issues that matter :* questions that are important. 6. *to harm :* nuire.

« We try not to treat him like a star, but I fear that despite that, he may turn into one. Already, I think he is looking at himself in the mirror a bit too much. »

Daily Mail, monday, october 26, 1992.

Record success : Jordy Lemoine, already at home in a sound studio.

QUESTIONS

I. Lire attentivement le document ci-joint.

II. Répondre aux questions suivantes en rédigeant des phrases complètes en anglais.

1. What sort of document is it ? Where does it come from ? When was it written (BEP 2 pts, CAP 3 pts) ?

2. Who is this document about (name and family-name – age – nationality) (BEP 2 pts, CAP 3 pts) ?

3. How old was he when he started to play music ? What did he first play music with (BEP et CAP, 2 pts) ?

4. Where precisely did he make his first recording (BEP 1 pt, CAP 2 pts) ?

5. Since when has he been successful in France (BEP 2 pts, CAP 1 pt) ?

6. Has his mother got a job ? Justify your answer (BEP 1 pt, CAP 2 pts).
7. Why do people criticize his parents (BEP 1 pt, CAP 2 pts) ?
8. How do his parents « make sure this success doesn't harm him for life » (BEP et CAP, 1 pt) ?
9. Do you think he has a normal life for a boy of his age ? Why ? Why not (BEP 3 pts, CAP 2 pts) ?
10. Essay : Would you like to be a star (pop-singer, movie-star, sportsman) ? Justify your answer (10 lines) (BEP 5 pts, CAP 2 pts).

Montpellier

21 THÈME ABORDÉ — SPÉCIALITÉS

Terrorisme — CAS/ACC

DANGER, BABY FOOD !

Your mother tells you to give dinner to your baby brother. You open a jar of baby food, and inside you find three small pieces of glass.

That's exactly what happened to many people in England recently. Two baby food companies were the victims of a dangerous and horrible form of terrorism : consumer terrorism. A criminal contaminated baby food and demanded £1 million in ransom money.

People from all over Britain reported more than 300 cases of baby food jars contaminated with glass, pins or poison. Some of the jars had menacing messages inside. But police don't know if all of the reports were justified.

Food manufacturers quickly took 100 million jars of suspect baby food out of the shops. « We wanted to react quickly, in the interests of consumers », said John Eyre, the director of a British supermarket chain. Manufacturers then replaced them with jars with tamper-proof packaging[1]. This permits consumers to see if the jar was opened before.

Consumer terrorism is not only extremely dangerous, it is also very expensive. It takes the police a lot of time and money to find the criminals. Manufacturing companies often prefer to destroy millions of uncontaminated products just because one or two were contaminated. This costs them a lot of money. If a product is poisoned, it gets a bad reputation : people won't buy it, and many workers then lose their jobs.

QUESTIONS

I. Right or wrong ? Justify your answer (BEP 5 pts, CAP 10 pts) :

1. A criminal contaminated baby food jars and asked for a lot of money to stop doing so.

1. *tamper proof packaging :* emballage qui permet à l'acheteur de vérifier que le produit n'a pas été ouvert.

2. The baby food companies couldn't do anything about it.
3. A few jars were taken out of the shops.
4. British supermarkets stopped selling baby food jars.
5. Manufacturing companies destroyed millions of uncontaminated jars.

II. Answer the questions (BEP 4 pts, CAP 4 pts) :

1. What happened recently to many people in England ?
2. What were the baby food jars contaminated with ?
3. What is John Eyre's job ?
4. How much did consumer terrorism cost to the companies ?

III. Essay (BEP 5 pts, CAP 3 pts) :

What are the consequences of consumer terrorism for consumers, society, food manufacturers ? Give details.

IV. Translate into french (BEP 6 pts, CAP 3 pts) :

« That's exactly what... were justified. »

Rennes

22

THÈME ABORDÉ — SPÉCIALITÉS

British people and holidays — Tertiaire

QUESTIONS

I. Étudiez attentivement les graphiques suivants et complétez les quatre textes après avoir bien lu l'énoncé de chaque exercice.

II. Questionnaire à choix multiple.

A. Frequency of holiday taking

1974		1984
44 %	1 holiday only	38 %
14 %	2 holidays	17 %
4 %	3 holidays	5 %
2 %	4 or more holidays	2 %
37 %	No holiday	38 %

B.

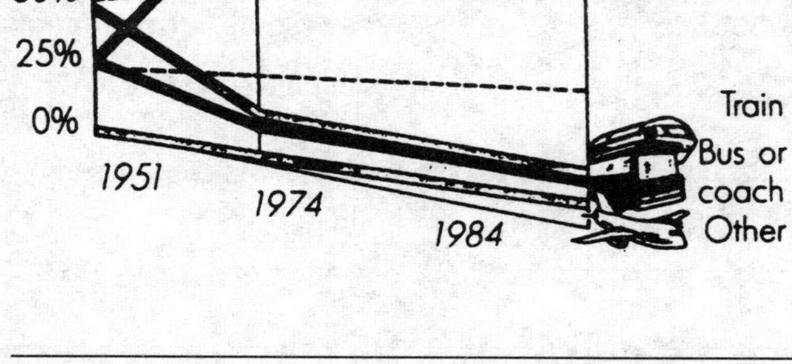

C. Hotel occupancy

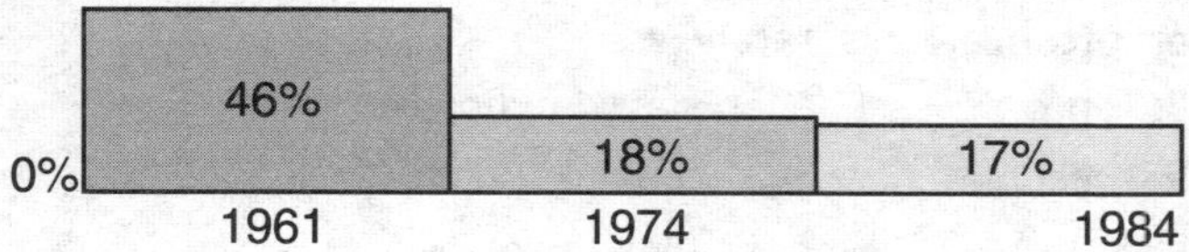

D.

Money spent on all tourism by UK residents (£m):

1974		*1984*
1,375	In England	4,525
1,800	In Britain	5,650
975	Overseas	5,300

1. Après avoir observé les graphiques A et B, vous compléterez le texte suivant de manière logique avec les données chiffrées ci-dessous (BEP 3 pts, CAP 5 pts) : four, thirty-eight, seventy, eight, 1951 :

.... years ago, in 1984, ... per cent of the British population did not go on holiday. Between 1974 and 1984 the proportion of people going .... times or more on holiday did not change. In .... nobody used the plane to travel in the same year, only 25 % of the population used the car to travel but in 1984 it represented more than .... per cent.

2. À partir du graphique A, choisissez le mot approprié dans la liste suivante (BEP 5 pts, CAP 2,5 pts) : very few, some, most, enough, a lot :

.... of people took no holiday in 1984 because they did not have money.

.... people in 1984 could take holidays twice a year.

.... people only took one holiday.

.... people went on holiday 4 times or more in 1984.

3. Après avoir étudié les graphiques A, B et C, complétez les phrases avec les adverbes suivants (BEP 2 pts, CAP 1 pt) :
never, often, always, rarely :

In 1861, people .... stayed in hotels.

In 1951, people .... took the plane.

In 1984, people .... took the plane.

In 1984, 38 % of the British population .... stayed at home.

4. A partir des graphiques A, B et D, complétez les phrases à l'aide des propositions suivantes (BEP 5 pts, CAP 1,5 pt) :
the cheapest, the least popular, more ... than, as many ... as, the most popular, the biggest :

In 1984, British people spend .... money .... in 1974.

.... sums of money were spent in Britain. The car was .... means of transport in 1984 and the plane was .... because it is certainly not .... way of travelling. In 1984, ... people went on holiday 4 times or more .... in 1974.

5. Cochez la bonne réponse (BEP 5 pts, CAP 10 pts) :

1) ❑ I smokes a lot.
❑ You
❑ He
❑ They

2) I want ❑ my pen.
❑ me
❑ mine
❑ I

3) ❑ Does he like music ?
❑ Do
❑ Is
❑ Are

4) He ❑ goes to school everyday.
❑ go
❑ is going
❑ going

5) « What's your ❑ shop ? » – « John ».
❑ car
❑ job
❑ name

6) Dogs don't like ❑ these cats.
❑ cats.
❑ the cats.
❑ a cat.

7) He went to Spain ❑ next week.
❑ tomorrow.
❑ tonight.
❑ two years ago.

8) The accident happened ❑ on 1989.
❑ in 1989.
❑ from 1989.
❑ at 1989.

9) « I like rugby » ❑ « I am ».
❑ « Neither do I ».
❑ « So do I ».
❑ « I didn't ».

10) « ❑ Did you read this book ? ». « No, I haven't ».
❑ Do
❑ Have
❑ Didn't

11) « How ❑ noisy is it ? » « It weighs 50 kilos ».
❑ comfortable
❑ wide
❑ heavy

12) There ❑ have two chairs in my bedroom.
❑ is
❑ are
❑ was

13) A lot of ❑ man came to your party.
❑ people
❑ person
❑ things

14) He has a gun in ❑ a left hand.
❑ his
❑ the
❑ this

15) « Where do you comme ❑ to ? » « Paris ».
❑ at
❑ from
❑ into

16) Susan lent me a very good book.
❑ Its book is about the USA.
❑ His
❑ A
❑ Her

17) ❑ Have you seen John ?
❑ Did
❑ Were
❑ Are

18) You're American, ❑ are you ?
❑ weren't you ?
❑ aren't you ?
❑ were you ?

19) Look, ❑ it rained.
❑ it rains.
❑ it was raining.
❑ it's raining.

20) He was born ❑ in the 15th of november 1992.
❑ at
❑ during
❑ on

CORRIGÉS

HÔTELLERIE-RESTAURATION

Corse

5

THÈME ABORDÉ — SPÉCIALITÉS

Les vins — Hôtellerie/Restauration

WINE DISTRICTS

I. Right or wrong ? Justify your answer :

1. No, sherry comes from the extreme south of Spain.
2. Yes, the Loire Valley produces Sancerre, Muscadet and other wines.
3. Not precisely. Oporto is the centre of the wine area but port wine comes from the area north of the town.
4. Certainly not. This famous French wine comes from the Burgundy wine district, just north of Lyon.
5. Wrong. Spain – apart from sherry – produces lighter table wines.

II. Put the following sentences in the interrogative form :

1. Does Peter go to the restaurant every sunday ?
2. Are you eating potatoes ?
3. Did they drink a pint of beer in a pub ?
4. Shall I go to the cinema with you ?
5. Would he like to order an apple-pie ?

III. Choose the right answer :

1. In August, I *went* to Paris.
2. My father told me that *there were* some apples on the table.
3. I have bought *four* different dresses.
4. I want *to* drink a glass of wine.
5. Tomorrow, we *will* buy a carpet.

IV. Put the verbs into the correct tense :

• *Aide grammaticale :* cet exercice est très précisément ciblé. Rappelez-vous que le présent simple s'emploie pour exprimer une action habituelle tandis que le présent continu indique que l'action est en train de se dérouler.

1. My mother always *makes* a cake for my birthday.
2. He can't come now. He is *doing* his homework.
3. He *watches* all the football matches on television.
4. *Are you going* to school already ?
5. Come and listen to the radio. The president *is speaking*.

V. Each of these sentences is the answer to a question. Write the questions :

• *Aide méthodologique :* on aura évidemment compris qu'il s'agit de retrouver la question qui a pu être posée pour conduire à chacune de ces réponses.

• *Aide grammaticale :* ces phrases sont toutes au SIMPLE PAST. Revoyez d'autre part les mots interrogatifs (1, 2, 3, 4).

1. Who did you see ? / Whom did you see ?
2. How many biscuits did they eat ?
3. Where did he meet her ?
4. What time did he arrive ?
5. Did he take a taxi ?

Lyon

6

THÈME ABORDÉ — SPÉCIALITÉS

Garçon de café — Hôtellerie/Restauration

THE HARD ROCK CAFÉ

I. Right/wrong :

1. Wrong. You often have to queue to get in.

2. Right.

3. Wrong. The Hard Rock Café is the most successful restaurant in the world.

4. Wrong. They help campaigns to protect the environment.

5. Right.

II. Make sentences with the following groups of words :

• *Aide méthodologique :* observer attentivement les éléments qui vous sont donnés. Ils sont en désordre, sans ponctuation (hormis un point d'interrogation) ni majuscule de début de phrase ; en revanche, tous les mots sont là pour vous aider à constituer une phrase correcte.

1. Can I reserve a table for lunch ?

2. The cost for this menu is £20.

3. Sorry : there is no butter left.

4. I will have a piece of Cheddar.

5. These is no pepper left on the table.

III. Poser les questions correspondant à la partie soulignée des phrases suivantes :

1. How much do you spend every month in restaurants ?

2. When do you finish your season ?

3. Why does the restaurant close in winter ?
4. How long have you been cooking ?
5. What is the chef's speciality ?

IV. Dialogue :

• *Aide méthodologique* : voir les formules de politesse.

– May I take your order ?
– I would like a café chef salad and a bar-b-que chicken.
– I'm afraid there is no chicken left, Sir. This dish has been very successful this evening.
– Never mind. Let's have a cheeseburger.
– I'm terribly sorry. This is very unusual, but we've run out of cheese.

V. Question à développer :

• *Aide méthodologique :* sur le fond et la forme, on trouvera des appuis utiles dans le texte.

• *Prérequis grammaticaux :*
– expression de la cause, de la préférence,
– mots de liaison (first, besides, secondly...).

• *Aide lexicale : atmosphere*, ambiance ; *surroundings*, cadre ; *exciting*, excitant ; *experience*, expérience ; *period*, période ; *friendly*, amical, chaleureux ; *tiring*, fatigant.

I would like to work in a Hard Rock Café, just for one or two years. It is probably an exalting experience.

You are given the chance of meeting young people and even famous stars. These restaurants are decorated with objects I like, and what's more, I could listen to the music I prefer, all day long. Besides, I approve of their campaign for the protection of nature.

On the other hand, working in such conditions must be exhausting.

Orléans-Tours

7

THÈME ABORDÉ — SPÉCIALITÉS

Serveur de restaurant — Hôtellerie/Restauration (BEP)
Restauration/Hébergement intégrés (CAP)

AT THE RESTAURANT

I. Regardez l'illustration et répondez aux questions suivantes en rédigeant des phrases complètes :

1. He is a client, or a guest.
He is sitting down.

2. He is a waiter.
He is standing up.

II. Imaginez deux répliques possibles du serveur :

1. I'm sorry, your steak will be coming right away.

2. I'm terribly sorry. Would you like something else while waiting ?

III. Pour chaque objet numéroté (sauf les n°s 7 et 9), rédigez une phrase pour le présenter en utilisant les tournures « There is/There are » :

1. There is a spoon.

2. There are knives.

3. There is a table-cloth.

4. There is an ashtray.

5. There are glasses.

6. There is a napkin.

7. There is a plate.

IV. A) En faisant des phrases complètes répondez aux questions ou posez les questions suivant le cas :

1. Where does it take place ?

2. What time is it ?

3. Service will start in 30 minutes.

4. She is worried about the bread.

5. What does a baker sell ?
6. It is because of the Wine and food Festival.
7. What is breakfast ?
8. People are tired of diets and light food.
9. How long has he been talking ?
10. Have you tasted the vegetable soup ?

B) En vous aidant du contexte, rayez les mauvaises réponses (a, b et c) :

1. un plat de viande
   It is the main course.
2. assaisonnement
   The seasoning of the soup is perfect.
3. progressé
   It's perfect : you have improved.
4. École d'hôtellerie et de restauration.

V. Faites correspondre les noms des plats à la description qui convient :

1. *b* ; **2.** *e* ; **3.** *a* ; **4.** *c* ; **5.** *d*.

VI. Répondez aux questions concernant le dessin ci-dessous en faisant des phrases complètes :

1. He is a cook.
2. He is working in the kitchen.
3. He is wearing a chef's hat.
4. a knife ; a grater ; a tin-opener ; a pot.

VII. Posez les questions correspondant aux réponses données :

1. Where is the rosé ?
2. Have you got various kinds of cheese ?
3. Could you bring me the bill, please ?

VIII. Écrivez en anglais à quelles parties d'un menu correspondent les plats mentionnés ci-dessous :

a starter ; a main course ; cheese ; dessert.

IX. Conjuguez le verbe entre parenthèses au temps qui convient :

- We went to the seaside last summer.
- He plays tennis every Monday.
- They have learnt the piano since the age of 5.
- Look ! She is crossing the street.

SECRÉTARIAT/BUREAUTIQUE

Amiens

8

THÈME ABORDÉ — SPÉCIALITÉS

Matériel traditionnel — Secteur tertiaire

SOUND IDEA

I. Répondez en anglais aux questions suivantes, non par de simples mots mais par des phrases complètes :

1. No, she doesn't work in a traditional office, she works at her home.
2. She has got four young children.
3. Business correspondents who phoned Laura Newman could hear typewrites clattering, telephones ringing, filing cabinets opening and shutting.
4. She recorded some typical office noises to project a good professional image on the phone.
5. The sound effects tape is sold at a price of $ 14.95.
6. The sort of people who are interested in such a tape are stay-at-home business people.
7.

(Il conviendra de traiter cette question A7 un peu plus longuement puisque 3 pts lui sont octroyés au niveau BEP.)

I would rather work in an office, because it offers you an opportunity to meet people, to improve your professional skills. In my view, working at home must be a bore, but some people accept it out of necessity... and bosses are sometimes so unpleasant...

II. En anglais, décrivez l'illustration en 4 à 5 lignes :

• *Aide méthodologique* : le candidat s'attachera moins à décrire l'environnement ménager – hormis l'essentiel – qu'à dire le contraste entre l'occupation professionnelle et les tâches domestiques.

• *Prérequis grammaticaux* :

– présent continu,

– expressiion de l'opposition (while – whereas),

– expression de la simultanéité (while – as soon as – as).

• *Aide lexicale* : rudiments du lexique bureautique et domestique.

Laura Newman is obviously in her fully equipped kitchen ; but actually, she is sitting over her office work. A typewriter is laid on the table, and Laura is answering the phone while a meal is stewing on the electric cooker. Happily, she has just switched on the cassette player and started the sound effects tape with prerecorded office noises.

III. Traduction des paragraphes 4 et 5 :

4. Newman a résolu le problème en enregistrant une série de bruits de bureau caractéristiques. Le résultat en est une bande d'effets sonores qui a si bien marché que Newman s'est lancée dans les affaires – la vendant à d'autres hommes d'affaires travaillant chez eux, au prix de 14,95 dollars.

5. Newman propose maintenant une seconde bande avec des bruits d'imprimantes et de terminaux d'ordinateurs. C'est pour les gens qui veulent que leurs correspondants téléphoniques pensent qu'ils sont entourés de machines actives.

Lille

9

THÈME ABORDÉ — Ordinateurs

SPÉCIALITÉS — Secteur tertiaire

A BYTE AT THE RESTAURANT

I. Répondez en anglais par des phrases complètes :

1. They were certainly teachers, since they used to work in school classrooms.
2. The Green Rooms is a restaurant.
3. Mr. Thomson met problems when a lot of customers asked for their bills at the same time.
4. He thought of computerized billing.
5. No, he wasn't quite satisfied with the accounts package he bought, because the program was too slow.
6. He wrote a billing program by himself.
7. No, he wasn't. He had no previous experience.
8. Mr Thomson is now considering converting his restaurant into a computer shop.

II. Décrivez l'illustration en 4 à 5 lignes :

• *Aide méthodologique :* il s'agit d'un travail descriptif sans surprise. Ne pas omettre l'arrière-plan, élément clé de la compréhension du texte.

• *Aide grammaticale :* revoir les adverbes, prépositions et locutions prépositionnelles indiquant le LIEU (*in front of/.., in the foreground, on the left/...*, etc.).

• *Aide lexicale :* voir le lexique de la bureautique à la fin de l'ouvrage.

This is a photograph of Mr Thomson in his restaurant. As a matter of fact, if you don't notice the tables which are set up in the background, you can get confused about Mr Thomson's activity. He is surrounded with a sophisticated equipment : a computer with its screen and its keyboard, a calculating machine…

III. Traduisez en français le paragraphe 5 :

L'affaire de conception de programmes s'accroît rapidement, de l'ordre de 80 000 livres par an, et le chiffre d'affaires du restaurant approche les 130 000 livres. Mais il n'y a pas de frais généraux dans l'affaire d'informatique, et le restaurant est en passe de devenir une activité secondaire, n'ouvrant que les vendredis et samedis soir. Mr. Thomson envisage même de convertir le restaurant en un magasin d'informatique.

Nice

10

THÈME ABORDÉ — SPÉCIALITÉS

Ordinateurs portables — CAS/ACC/ESAC

TOSHIBA NOTEBOOKS.

I. Répondez aux questions en anglais :

1. This is a portable notebook computer.
2. The advertiser is Toshiba, a company which is the leader in portable computing.
3. A young lady (A) is sitting at her desk. She wears glasses and looks about thirty. Maybe she is typing a letter for her boss.
4. She may be a secretary or a receptionnist.
5. These Toshiba computers are full-featured and portable.

II. Traduisez :

1. More and more people use computers.
2. Did they have the situation fully in hand ?
3. Wherever he goes, he doesn't forget his computer.
4. Does she count on their support ?

III. Essai (BEP seulement) :

• *Aide méthodologique :* même si l'aspect positif doit largement dominer, il est toujours judicieux d'examiner les revers de toute découverte technologique.

• *Prérequis grammaticaux :*

– expression de la cause *(because, since, owing to, because of...)*,

– passé révolu (habitude avec *used to*),

– expression de l'opposition.

• *Aide lexicale :* se reporter au lexique de la bureautique à la fin de l'ouvrage.

Computers have considerably changed office work. In a few seconds, they can perform certain tasks which used to take a lot of time. Computers can be applied to many functions such as : word processing, graphics, calculations, data bases... Their size of memory is extremely useful.

Unfortunately, there are some drawbacks. Computers tend to procure unemployment since a computer can replace several employees, and in my personal opinion, they tend to diminish personal involvement.

Grenoble

11

THÈME ABORDÉ — Répondeurs téléphoniques

SPÉCIALITÉS — Secteur tertiaire

TALKING TELEPHONES

I. Répondre en anglais aux questions suivantes :

1. Today, people have telephones everywhere : they can even telephone from their car, or from the street. Ten years ago, they had only one telephone at home, and one in the office.
2. An answerphone enables its owner to record phone calls as he or she is out.
3. Callers have difficulties in formulating the right message in a short time. Owners meet problems too, because they have to make a good impression on their correspondents.
4. Life is easier since the telephone was invented. The telephone saves time and makes people closer.

II. Traduction du premier paragraphe :

Il y a dix ans, les gens avaient un téléphone à la maison et un au bureau. Aujourd'hui, les gens ont des téléphones partout : à la maison, dans la voiture, dans le jardin. On voit même des gens se promener dans les rues avec des téléphones sans fil.

III. Posez la question portant sur les mots soulignés :

1. When did people have one telephone in the house ?
2. What does he quickly put down ?

IV. Transformez la structure verbale en fonction de l'indicateur de temps :

1. In the future, people will have telephones everywhere.
2. If he was discouraged, he would quickly put down the receiver.

V. Essay :

• *Aide méthodologique :* ne pas se compliquer inutilement la tâche en rédigeant un texte au style indirect, mais respecter scrupuleusement la consigne en utilisant le style direct ; le jury de correction attendra sans doute du candidat la formulation en toutes lettres du numéro de téléphone, c'est-à-dire, comme il se dirait.

• *Aide grammaticale :*

– formules téléphoniques élémentaires,

– formules de politesse,

– verbes de volonté + proposition infinitive,

– date, heure, âge.

• *Aide lexicale :*

– nombres ordinaux et cardinaux.

« Hello, Mike, this is Graeme speaking. It's a pity you are out. We are having a party to celebrate the centenary of my birth ! ... Of course, I'm joking. Actually, I will be twenty on June 20th (the twentieth). We would like you to join us at my house, at 8.30 p.m. (eight thirty). Please call me back to confirm your coming. Don't forget to write down my new phone number : 92.90.44.15 (nine two, nine o, double four, one five). Let me hear from you soon. »

Corse

12 THÈME ABORDÉ — SPÉCIALITÉS

Activités de secrétariat — CAS/ACC/ESAC

DEAR SIR

I. Right or wrong ? Justify your answer when it is wrong :

1. **Wrong.**
   No, she doesn't. She says she made a terrible mistake when she became a secretary.
2. **Right.**
3. **Wrong.**
   She has to answer the phone because her three bosses are always too busy.
4. **Wrong.**
   No, she doesn't. She often has to type some extra letters before leaving.
5. **Wrong.**
   A secretary is not allowed to get angry.

II. Choose the correct word to complete each sentence :

1. It's their computer.
2. I look forward to hearing from you.
3. Have you been to London before ?
4. Whose typewriter is that ?
5. It's on monday morning.

III. Write the past participle of the verbs in these sentences :

1. The desk was broken.
2. I have not sent the telex yet.
3. Have you seen him before ?

IV. Write the comparatives of the adjectives in these sentences :

1. This photocopier is easier to use than that one.
2. John earns less money than Peter.
3. My boss is more intelligent than you.

V. Put the following sentences into the interrogative form :

1. Is it going to take a week ?
2. Did they close it last december ?
3. Must she leave early today ?
4. Has she got a new typewriter ?

VI. Choose the right tense :

1. He always drives to work.
2. At the moment they are typing.
3. I did not go to work, yesterday.
4. I will be able to take shorthand, next year.

Nantes

13

THÈME ABORDÉ — SPÉCIALITÉS

Carte de client privilégié — Tertiaire/Alimentation/Hôtellerie

HARRODS ACCOUNT CARD

1. Harrods is situated in Knightbridge, a central district of London.

2. There are dozens of different departments in the store.

3. We can find a great variety of items at Harrods', whether you are after a CD, or cat food, or a bottle of wine.

4. The Harrods Account Card can be very useful for busy persons.

5. With the Account Card, special invitations and the famous catalogues are sent.

6. You simply order the items you need, by phone.

7. Delivery is free within the central London delivery area.

8. You are informed concerning special Christmas sales, by the famous Harrods catalogue.

9. No, they probably don't, because this advertisement focuses on everyday items and it doesn't mention more expensive purchases.

10. You have to complete the Application form and send it by post.

11.

> • *Aide méthodologique :* attention au barème qui seul vous indique le statut un peu particulier de cette question qui équivaut à un essai, par conséquent à un développement plus important. Cependant, les données de votre réponse sont probablement contenues dans le texte : cela vous facilite la tâche de formulation.

Such a card is very convenient because you can order by phone the items you have selected from the catalogue. You can benefit from special promotions and within a central London area you can take advantage of free delivery. Harrods card holders are regularly informed by guide, catalogues or invitations.

THÈMES GÉNÉRAUX

Poitiers

14

THÈME ABORDÉ — SPÉCIALITÉS

Argent de poche — CAS/ACC/ESAC

BRITISH BANKS

I. Right or wrong ? (Justifier en citant le texte) :

1. Wrong. Timothy is 16, and Wendy 14.

2. Wrong. Timothy found a part-time job at a McDonald's restaurant.

3. Right. He and his parents were pleased.

4. Right. Anne said it's extremely important for young people to understand... that we usually work quite hard to get it.

5. Wrong. He promised to put part of his salary in the bank each week.

6. Wrong. He promised to put it... each week.

7. Right. Bill thought the price was scandalous.

8. Right. Is it right for their son to be able to buy something when it goes against their principles ?

9. Wrong. He doesn't contribute financially at all to the family.

10. Right. Anne and Bill are worried because they are in fact contributing to the destruction of important values.

II. Poser des questions sur les éléments soulignés :

1. Where do Bill and Anne live ?

2. Who do they live with ?

3. How old is Timothy ?

4. What did Timothy find ?

5. How long has he had his job ?

6. How often will he put part of his salary in the bank ?

7. How much was his pair of jeans ?

8. How far is the bank from Timothy's house ?

III. Essay : Talking about pocket money :

• *Aide méthodologique* : l'énoncé du sujet vous propose sous forme de questions précises diverses pistes qui sont plus suggérées qu'imposées. Il paraît, en effet, difficile de répondre sérieusement à chacune, en moins de soixante mots pour l'ensemble. Sur le fond, votre réaction à l'attitude des parents de Timothée sera sans aucun doute intéressante, mais constituera une voie linguistique plus difficile à suivre.

• *Prérequis grammaticaux* :

– exression de l'obligation morale et du devoir (MUST / SHOULD / OUGHT TO / HAVE TO),

– expression du conditionnel (irréel du présent) (irréel du passé).

• *Aide lexicale* : voir le vocabulaire relatif à l'argent et celui relatif au comportement et à la morale, en fin d'ouvrage.

I can understand Timothy's parents' reaction. They had encouraged their son to earn his own money to make him more conscious. When Timothy asked his parents for £80 to buy a jeans – which is awfully expensive–, it was the very occasion not to abandon their principles. Bill was right. Timothy had to experience by himself the consequence of an unreasonable spending.

The problem with pocket money is that it can make you used to manage certain expenses such as a motorbike maintenance, petrol, CDs and so on, but it rarely makes you aware of everyday spendings.

Strasbourg

15

THÈME ABORDÉ | SPÉCIALITÉS

Désertification rurale | ACC/CAS/Distribution-Magasinage/ESAC

THERE'S NOTHING TO KEEP YOUNGSTERS HERE

I. Juste ou faux ? Si l'élément souligné est faux, rayez-le et notez la bonne réponse en dessous, telle qu'elle figure dans le texte :

1. **Juste.**
2. **Faux.** It is set on a hillside at 1,000 ft.
3. **Faux.** Its population is falling.
4. **Faux.** It is now 12.5 per cent.
5. **Faux.** Tourism is flourishing.
6. **Faux.** Many of them have moved away.
7. **Juste.**

II. Find in the text three reasons why young people leave the town of Alston :

1. The iron foundry closed and the unemployment rate shot up to 37 per cent.
2. There is nothing for young people to stay for : there is no longer a market.
3. The rural side of life is threatened, because upland farming is no longer viable.

III. À partir des informations contenues dans le texte, complétez les phrases :

There aren't many young people in Alston because there isn't much to do in this town. A lot of old people live there. The means of transportation are limited as there are no trains and only a few buses every day.

IV. Posez la question pour laquelle l'élément souligné est la réponse :

1. Why do many young people leave ?
2. When did the butcher's shop go into liquidation ?
3. How many engineering companies have they got ?
4. How far is Penrith ?

V. Trouvez dans le texte les phrases de sens équivalent :

1. Alston is struggling for survival.
2. The unemployment rate shot up.
3. Alston suffers from its remote position.

VI. Répondez en anglais
– en six lignes minimum pour le BEP,
– en quatre lignes minimum pour le CAP :

Would you prefer to live in a city or in the country ? Say why.

• *Aide méthodologique :* cet énoncé vous invite clairement à un développement personnel fondé sur la comparaison de deux univers différents. La structuration en deux paragraphes semble naturelle, appuyée sur les caractères lexicaux et grammaticaux cités au-dessus.

• *Aide grammaticale :*

– Revoir les comparatifs d'infériorité et de supériorité :

– *more* [adj. long] *than...*
– [adj. court]-er than...
– *less... than...*

– Revoir l'expression de l'opposition :

but, in spite of (+ nom), *while* : tandis que, *however* : cependant, *although, though* : bien que, *on the contrary.*

– Emploi conseillé du présent simple (actif ou passif) puisque les idées concernant la ville ou la campagne définissent des états habituels.

• *Aide lexicale :*

tube ; rush-hour ; traffic jams ; pollution ; overcrowded ; to concentrate ; dirty, filthy ; space ; quietness, quiet ; picturesque ; means of transportation ; cultural activities ; convenient ; pleasant ; enjoyable.

I am particularly fond of nature. However, I would rather live in a city than live in the country, because town life is far more convenient. Nowadays, rural areas are almost deserted and young people have great difficulties in finding a job. Schools, banks, railway services are often suppressed ; even buses are getting scarcer and scarcer.

I admit cities are unhealthy, noisy and polluted. Inhabitants are nervous and violence is increasing. Nevertheless, you can take advantage of many facilities.

Polynésie française

16

THÈME ABORDÉ — SPÉCIALITÉS

Absentéisme dans l'entreprise — Tous BEP/CAP rénovés

KEEPING THE WORKERS AT WORK

I. Compréhension. Choose the right answer :

1. For the Australian Company « Goodyear », the main problem is :
c) absenteism.

2. In Australia people will be given prizes if :
b) they don't miss a day for any reason at all.

3. If they come to work regularly people will win :
c) 12 000 Australian dollars in ready cash.

4. The company has tried :
b) to have piped music throughout the factory.

II. Grammar. Find the questions corresponding to the answers :

1. What is the biggest concern for Goodyear ?

2. What did Goodyear begin a campaign against ?

3. What can they get when they work regularly ?

4. How will they make people happy at work ?

III. Translation

1. Translate into French :

Il y eut une lettre remise en main propre à tous les employés expliquant que, s'ils ne manquaient pas un jour pour quelque raison que ce soit, ils gagneraient un prix.

2. Translate into English :

Absenteism seems to be caused by different factors.

Good workers will qualify for a prize if they come to work regularly.

IV. Rédaction en anglais (8 à 10 lignes) : why is absenteism a real problem for a company ?

• *Aide méthodologique :* si le sujet n'est pas des plus faciles, il faut convenir, en revanche, que le concepteur guide rigoureusement le candidat tant dans le cheminement de ses idées que sur le terrain linguistique, en formulant quelques expressions spécialisées.

• *Prérequis grammaticaux :*

- rapports cause/conséquence,
- conseil (*should, have to...*),
- suggestion (*may...*).

• *Aide lexicale :* se référer au lexique des conditions de travail et des relations dans l'entreprise en fin de l'ouvrage.

Companies are rightly concerned with absenteism, for one reason at least : sick days certainly slow down production dramatically. As a matter of fact, managers cannot replace missing employees immediately. Consequently, there is a lack of a necessary link in the chain. Colleagues will be overworking soon and get tired quicker. The missing worker will lose confidence in himself or herself. Colleagues and bosses will tend to trust him no more.

The creation of better working conditions can help solve this big problem. Offices and workrooms should be more attractive. Time should be organised with flexible working hours.

Orléans-Tours

17 THÈME ABORDÉ — SPÉCIALITÉS

Travail saisonnier — CAS/ACC/Distribution-Magasinage/ESAC

WORKING HOLIDAYS

I. Compréhension :

1. Parmi les trois titres suivants, lequel pourrait convenir au texte ? Cochez la réponse correcte :

– Working holiday in Europe ☒

2. Relevez dans le texte les expressions correspondant aux définitions ci-dessous :

a) Unemployment.

b) Fruit-pickers.

c) A sleeping-bag.

d) At the bookshop.

e) Seasonal work.

3. Dites si les affirmations sont exactes (right) ou fausses (wrong), et justifiez par des expressions tirées du texte dans les deux cas :

a) **Wrong.** Often they can only afford a working holiday.

b) **Right.** There is unemployment everywhere in Europe now.

c) **Wrong.** Four or five guides are published every year.

d) **Wrong.** They can go there or ask their friends.

e) **Right.** These are the two main sorts of seasonal work.

f) **Wrong.** Cherries are picked two months before.

g) **Wrong.** Some farmers don't give you anywhere to live.

h) **Right.** You can spend several days looking hard.

i) **Right.** It's hard, but it can be worth it.

j) **Wrong.** They'd better find out as much as they can.

II. Compétence linguistique :

1. Posez la question correspondant à l'élément souligné de la phrase :

a) How often are guides published ?

b) What do they know about ?

c) Where did they find jobs ?

d) Who will she go with ?

e) What has he left home ?

2. Relevez deux superlatifs dans le texte (BEP et CAP), puis traduisez-les (BEP seulement) :

a) the most important differences = les différences les plus importantes

b) the safest thing = la chose la plus sûre

3. Conjuguez les verbes au temps qui convient après avoir observé les repères de temps :

a) They bought a new guide last week.
b) He will pick fruit next summer.
c) He goes to France every summer.

III. Production (60 mots) :

• *Aide méthodologique :* l'énoncé du sujet est fait d'un questionnement précis qui doit vous guider. Remarquez qu'il ne s'agit plus forcément d'emploi pendant les périodes de vacances scolaires.

• *Prérequis grammaticaux :*

– expression du souhait,
– expression du conditionnel (irréel du présent).

• *Aide lexicale :*

– noms de métier (voir en fin d'ouvrage) ; monde du travail.

I would certainly enjoy working in Great Britain, because I would like to improve the only foreign language I have been taught. To me, working as an au pair girl is all right, for several reasons. First, I am used to look after children ; secondly, I would have the feeling of being useful by teaching them some French. At last, this is the sort of job which enables you to stay a whole year.

Caen

18

THÈME ABORDÉ — SPÉCIALITÉS

Aide humanitaire — CAS/ACC/ESAC + Arts de la dentelle

A FRENCH DOCTOR IN ENGLISH-SPEAKING AFRICA

I. Compréhension :

1. Geneviève was an intern in a hospital in Quimper.
2. She decided to spend five weeks in Armenia because a doctor friend asked her to participate in the emergency aid mission « SOS Arménie ».
3. Her main task in Africa was to help the people who had fled the massacres by providing nourishment, clean water and by vaccinating children.
4. She used English, Zulu and Chichewa dialect.

II. Reporting her experience :

1. Her fondest memory is the day when Nelson Mandela was liberated. She was as overjoyed as black people.
2. Her sadest memory was the death of a one-year-old child they hadn't seen immediately, because they had taken an extra fifteen-minute rest.

III. Personal expression (BEP seulement) :

Premier sujet

• *Aide méthodologique :* sur le fond, réfléchir, bien sûr, à la nécessité de l'information dans un monde où les nations dépendent les unes des autres, qu'elles le veuillent ou non ; mais aussi à la nature et à la qualité de l'information, aux devoirs moraux qui en découlent.

• *Aide grammaticale :*

– expression de la cause, de la finalité et de la conséquence,
– expression de la volonté,
– voix passive.

• *Aide lexicale :* voir le lexique des droits de l'homme et celui des catastrophes naturelles, à la fin de l'ouvrage.

In this world of high technology, it is apparently easy to be informed about what is going on, all over the world. And indeed, information is of vital importance.

The problem today has become not to mix up information and sensationalism. At meal times, news programmes serve us our daily emotions. We must not get used to it. Knowledge should breed action.

Let us demand accurate information because it will enable us to urge authorities, to associate and carry out actions.

Deuxième sujet

• *Aide méthodologique* : ne pas limiter les idées au goût pour le dépaysement ou l'exotisme, à coup sûr légitimes, mais considérer également l'intérêt professionnel d'une telle expérience.

• *Aide grammaticale* :

– conditionnel,
– comparatifs d'infériorité, de supériorité,
– expression du but.

• *Aide lexicale* :

abroad, à l'étranger ; *different (from),* différent de ; *to make a difference,* changer ; *experience,* expérience ; *experienced,* expérimenté ; *far (from),* loin de ; *unemployment,* emploi ; *wages, salary,* salaire ; *to earn,* gagner (salaire).

Working abroad is probably a thrilling experience. First, it is certainly the best way of discovering a country and meeting its natives. Organised tours often offer us conventional images. But living and working among its inhabitants should give us a deeper knowledge.

After working for some years, I would like to go to a developing country and share my experience there with young people.

Anyway, working in a foreign country sometimes proves to be the best way of finding a job. Besides (since you are given extra bonuses), salaries are often higher.

III. Translate (CAP seulement) :

J'étais interne dans un hôpital de Quimper lorsqu'un ami médecin me demanda de participer à la mission d'aide d'urgence « SOS Arménie », afin d'aider les victimes du tremblement de terre de 1989. J'ai passé cinq semaines en Arménie et j'ai appris à quel point une main tendue et un peu de chaleur humaine pouvaient être importants dans les urgences médicales. Je suis revenue en France pour finir ma thèse, et je me suis immédiatement portée volontaire pour une mission avec Médecins sans Frontières en Afrique du Sud, ensuite huit mois plus tard au Malawi.

Lyon

19 THÈME ABORDÉ — SPÉCIALITÉS

Vedettariat — BEP/CAP tertiaires

« AIR » JORDAN

I. Imagine you are a reporter interviewing Michael Jordan. Ask him 10 questions about the following items.

Write down Michael's answers using his CV :

1. What's your name ?
My name is Michael Jeffrey Jordan.

2. What's your nickname ?
My nickname is Air Jordan.

3. When were you born ?
I was born on February 17th, 1963.

4. Where were your born ?
I was born in New York city.

5. What's your nationality ?
I'm American.

6. How tall are you ?
I am six feet, six inches tall.

7. What's your occupation ?
I'm a professional basketball player.

8. Which team do you play with ?
I play with the Chicago Bulls.

9. What's your uniform number ?
It's twenty-three.

10. How many letters do you receive each month ?
I receive 23,000 letters a month.

II. Answer the questions :

1. Jordan was given this nickname because he jumps very high.
2. His enormous success sometimes makes his life unpleasant.
3. Each time he walks down the street, he attracts a crowd. When he goes to the cinema, he has to enter a few minutes late and leave earlier so that the other spectators won't recognize him. He sometimes wears disguises.
4. Michael Jordan wears disguises because he doesn't want to be recognized. Unfortunately, he is so tall that people often guess who he is.

III. Essay : would you like to be famous ?

• *Aide méthodologique :* le texte donne quelques éléments utiles au plan lexical et grammatical. On s'attachera à montrer les aspects positifs et négatifs de la célébrité.

• *Aide grammaticale :* voir le conditionnel (irréel du présent), l'expression de la conséquence et de la finalité ; *must/should* (devoir).

• *Aide lexicale :*

to be surrounded with, être entouré de ; *to congratulate,* féliciter ; *unknown,* inconnu ; *a champion,* un champion ; *glory,* gloire ; *loneliness,* solitude.

Being famous means you have done something extraordinary. I certainly would like to. But, if you are a star, you have to deserve this favour. You must be a model of honesty and courtesy. You should not forget your privileges when so many people are unemployed and never listened to.

However, success can interfere with your own private life. Stars are regularly assaulted by reporters or surrounded with excited fans. Fame and glory do not necessarily keep loneliness away.

Glossaire

Thèmes :

MÉTIERS / MONDE DU TRAVAIL

a salary, wages	un salaire
to earn	gagner (un salaire)
part-time	temps partiel
full-time	plein temps
extra hours	heures supplémentaires
a canteen	une cantine
board and lodging	le logement et la nourriture
a pay sheet	une fiche de paie
temporary	temporaire
an employee	un employé
a clerk	un employé (banque, administr.)
a receptionnist	une réceptionniste
a chambermaid	une femme de chambre
a waiter, a waitress	un serveur, une serveuse
a salesman, a salesgirl	un vendeur, une vendeuse
an assistant	un vendeur, employé, commis, auxiliaire
a hand	un manœuvre
manpower	la main-d'œuvre
employment	l'emploi
unemployment (-ed)	chômage, chômeur
to dismiss someone	renvoyer quelqu'un
a workshop, workroom	un atelier

CONDITIONS DE TRAVAIL / RELATIONS DANS L'ENTREPRISE

timetable	horaire, grille horaire
punctual	ponctuel
nervousness	nervosité
surroundings	environnement
to relax	se détendre

relaxation	détente, relâchement, repos
space	espace, place
site	emplacement
to pollute	polluer
chemicals	produits chimiques
exhausted	épuisé
disease, illness	maladie
efficient	efficace
efficiency	efficacité
productive	productif
tense (-ness)	tendu (relation), tension
relationship	rapports humains
situation	situation
to optimize	améliorer
to reduce, to diminish	réduire
to cause	provoquer, entraîner
to sack	congédier (familier : virer)
to dismiss	renvoyer, démissionner
understanding	entente

SECRÉTARIAT / BUREAUTIQUE

office	bureau (pièce)
to enter	entrer (des données)
data base	base de données
to display	afficher
to type	taper, écrire à la machine
keyboard	clavier
word processing	traitement de texte
graphics	grapheur
memory	mémoire
software	logiciel
to file	classer
filing-cabinet	classeur (meuble)
a desk	un bureau (meuble)
a directory	un annuaire, un répertoire
a typewriter	une machine à écrire
a photocopier	un photocopieur

an answerphone	un répondeur téléphonique
chart	tableau, diagramme
circular	circulaire
to duplicate	reproduire
a dictating machine	un dictaphone
a fax machine	un télécopieur

VENTE

an item *an article*	un article
a purchase (to)	un achat
to buy from	acheter à
a salesman, salesgirl *a shop-assistant*	vendeur, vendeuse
a customer	client (achat)
a client	client (service)
to pay for something	payer quelque chose
a cashier, cash desk	caissier, caisse
to order	commander
a department	rayon (d'un grand magasin)
a bill	facture
a receipt	ticket de caisse, reçu
a brand	marque
a make	marque (de fabrique)
bulk buying	achat en gros
a retailer	détaillant
cost (to)	coût
wholesaler	grossiste
to deliver	livrer
including VAT	TVA incluse
instalment	un versement partiel

ARGENT / BANQUE

to save money	épargner, économiser
savings	économies

a cheque-book	un chéquier
a credit card	une carte de crédit
a bank account	un compte en banque
to cash a cheque	encaisser un chèque
to draw money	retirer de l'argent
available	disponible
overdraft	découvert
to owe	devoir (de l'argent)
interest rate	taux d'intérêt
a grant	une bourse (d'études), une aide
to grant a loan	accorder un prêt
cheap	bon marché
high-priced, expensive	cher
instalment	versement partiel
a coin	une pièce de monnaie
a banknote	un billet de banque
to spend, spent, spent	dépenser
to run into debts	s'endetter
to waste	gaspiller
thrifty	économe *(adj.)*
a spendthrift	un prodigue, dépensier

RESTAURATION

restaurant with a terrace	restaurant en terrasse
à la carte menu	menu à la carte
to set the table	dresser la table
to lay the table	mettre la table
today's special	plat du jour
local dish	plat régional
gourmet menu	menu gastronomique
hors d'œuvre, appetizer	hors-d'œuvre
main course	plat principal
home-made	fait maison
extra-charge	en supplément
dessert	dessert
cheese	fromage
spices	épices

pepper	poivre
vegetables	légumes
meat	viande
vinegar	vinaigre
oil	huile
fish	poisson
to boil	bouillir
to fry	frire
to peel	peler
rare	saignant
well-done	bien cuit
medium	à point
to simmer	mijoter
to roast	rôtir
raw	cru
light cooking	cuisine légère
to melt	fondre
ice cube	glaçon
on the rocks	avec des glaçons
to pour	verser
still water	eau plate
sparkling water	eau gazeuse
decaffeinated coffee	café décaféiné
black, white coffee	café noir, au lait
alcoholic drinks	boissons alcoolisées
soft drinks	boissons non alcoolisées
sparkling wine	vin mousseux
vintage	millésime
aperitives	apéritifs
chilled	frais
ice-cold	glacé
at room temperature	chambré
game	gibier
pasta	pâtes
trolley	table roulante
headwaiter	maître d'hôtel

HÔTELLERIE

accommodation	logement
facilities	aménagement
room charge	prix de la chambre
single room	chambre pour 1 personne
double room	chambre à 1 lit pour 2 personnes
shower and toilet	douche et WC
to share	partager
twin room	chambre à 2 lits
without bath	sans bain
youth hostel	auberge de jeunesse
four-star hotel	hôtel 4 étoiles
inn	auberge
quiet	calme
spacious	spacieux
vacant	libre
available	disponible
sea view	vue mer
luggage (sg.)	bagages
to carry	porter
travel bag	sac de voyage
suitcase	valise
briefcase	mallette
trunk	malle
rucksack	sac à dos
soap	savon
shampoo	shampooing
bin	poubelle
guest	client
coat-hanger	cintre
coat-rack	portemanteau (mural)
socket	prise électrique
air-conditioned	à conditionnement d'air
radiator	radiateur
TV lounge	salle de TV
arrival	arrivée
departure	départ
length of stay	durée de séjour

to vacate a room	libérer une chambre
full-board	pension complète
half-board	demi-pension
sheet	drap
pillow	oreiller
blanket	couverture
mattress	matelas
bath towel	serviette de bain
wardrobe	penderie
room rate	prix de la chambre
bill totals	totalité des dépenses

MORALE / COMPORTEMENT

to allow	permettre
to prohibit	prohiber, interdire (loi, règlement)
to forbid, forbade, forbidden	interdire
to cheat	tricher
to deceive	tromper
honest	honnête
dishonest	malhonnête
shameful, shame	honteux, honte
truth, true	la vérité, vrai
grateful	reconnaissant
false	faux
lazy	paresseux
industrious	travailleur
to forgive	pardonner
to avoid	éviter
to pretend	faire semblant
to bully	brutaliser, malmener
to relieve	soulager
a relief	un soulagement
a lie (to–)	un mensonge (mentir)
a liar	un menteur
courage, courageous	courage, courageux
brave	courageux

AIDE HUMANITAIRE / DROITS DE L'HOMME / CATASTROPHES NATURELLES

to starve	mourir de faim
starvation	famine
hunger	faim
to die	mourir
disease	maladie
to lack	manquer de
victim	victime
to slaughter (a–) *to massacre (a–)*	massacrer (un massacre)
a cease-fire	cessez-le-feu
to protect	protéger
human rights	droits de l'homme
to violate	violer, enfreindre (la loi)
to wound	blesser
to kill	tuer
to torture	torturer
to defend	défendre
to prohibit	interdire (loi)
to abolish	abolir
a disaster	un désastre
a catastrophe	une catastrophe
earthquake	tremblement de terre
flood *inundation*	inondation
drought	sécheresse
vulcano eruption	éruption volcanique
to rescue	porter secours
to save	sauver

OPINION / ARGUMENTATION

to believe	croire
to agree (with)	être d'accord
to disagree (with)	être en désaccord
to approve of	approuver

to be right	avoir raison
to be wrong	avoir tort
to share	partager
to consider	considérer, envisager
to feel that	avoir le sentiment que
to point out	faire remarquer
according to	selon
unlike	à la différence de
in my opinion	à mon avis
from my point of view	selon mon point de vue
to contradict	contredire
to be against	être contre
to be for	être pour
idea	idée
opinion	opinion
contradictory	contradictoire
fact	fait
opposition, conflict	opposition, conflit
to struggle against	lutter contre
to support	soutenir

Achevé d'imprimer sur les presses de
l'Imprimerie Hérissey à Évreux
Dépôt légal : 6155 - Octobre 1993
N° d'imprimeur : 63271

50-